Praise for *Grow with the Flow*

"Katie's honest and moving memoir talks with vim and humor about making the absolute most of what life throws at you. An inspiration for so many of us."

—YASSMIN ABDEL-MAGIED
engineer and author of *Yassmin's
Story* and *You Must Be Layla*

"Most people support inclusion conceptually. Katie lives and breathes it, while modeling a roadmap for other leaders who want to dominate a marketplace, live a more purposeful life, and face fears head on. This is not just a book on tackling the energy challenge. It's an inspirational story about how to think creatively to make a big dream come true."

—LORI FELDMAN
chief executive officer

"*Grow with the Flow* is a bible for success. Katie reveals how we can override the voice in our head that tells us not to try because we aren't ready. We will never be 100 percent ready. Seize every opportunity in your life and watch how many new opportunities will spring up every single day."

—RUCHI SHARMA
Lean In Women at Work leader

"Katie's personality and passion make this book a compelling call to action. Katie is a perfect example of the saying 'actions speak louder than words.' She will inspire you to work through challenges and emerge stronger than you were before."

—MAYBELYN H. PLECIC
professional services manager in Presidio
Lean In Wonder Women leader/author

"Katie is a powerhouse of energy—a woman of grit, determination, and dedication. This book is a peek into what it takes to be a badass, bold woman who runs with the wolves yet be vulnerable at times."

—PAYEL MITRA
founder and president,
Lean In Sustainability

"*Grow with the Flow* is unfiltered, raw, vulnerable, and hilarious. This book is a roadmap that shows how to turn challenging situations into opportunities. It exposes toxic mindsets, work cultures, and behaviors that prevent growth, and gives you the tools to overcome those challenges to thrive."

—RITA HAUSKEN
strategist and leadership coach
founder of Shestainability
Lean In energy leader

"Katie Mehnert's story is about much more than persevering through devastation after a historic flood. It's about innovating and helping to revolutionize a massive industry while also rebuilding a family's life. In *Grow with the Flow*, readers will see why so many people have joined Katie's movement, why she was invited to testify before Congress, and why learning to frame your desired outcomes can be life-changing."

—JOSH LEVS
author of *All In*, winner of
the Nautilus Gold Award

"This is Katie Mehnert: raw and unfiltered doing what she does best—putting herself on the public stage and sharing her experiences. *Grow with the Flow* is an extension of what she set out to do after leaving the corporate world to start her own company, Pink Petro, and enduring the ups and downs unique to entrepreneurs in order to create a better, more equal culture in the energy industry. With this book, Mehnert has written her manifesto."

—REBECCA PONTON
author of *Breaking the GAS Ceiling:*
Women in the Offshore Oil & Gas Industry

"Katie's stories of survival, growth through hardship, and tenacious grit will have you cheering and fist-pumping your way through each chapter. We all face personal and professional demons, and Katie shows how recognizing them is the first step to conquering them. This is an inspirational read on how to be optimistic about what life throws at you so you too can Grow with the Flow."

—AMANDA BARLOW
geologist and author

"What a vulnerable and authentic story about privilege, tragedy, and humility. We need more leaders like Katie Mehnert, who are selfless and resilient, to show more women and girls that it's okay to be fierce and powerful. The world is counting on us to use our resources to create a positive impact. Katie Mehnert's story is an example of how the universe works. When we are givers and expect nothing in return, then it delivers."

—JULENE ALLEN
founder/CEO of Women of
Color in the Workplace

GROW WITH THE FLOW

GROW WITH THE FLOW

EMBRACE DIFFERENCE, OVERCOME FEAR, AND PROGRESS WITH PURPOSE

KATIE MEHNERT

Minneapolis

Hardcover ISBN-13: 978-1-63489-323-7
Paperback ISBN-13: 978-1-63489-318-3

Library of Congress Catalog Number: 2020902927
Printed in the United States of America
First Printing: 2020

24 23 22 21 20   5 4 3 2 1

Cover design by Steve Leard
Interior design by Patrick Maloney

Wise Ink Creative Publishing
807 Broadway St NE
Suite 46
Minneapolis, MN, 55413

To order, visit www.itascabooks.com or call 1-800-901-3480. Reseller discounts available.

To my husband, Mark, who says "I do" every day,
and to my daughter, Ally, who sparkles plenty.

CONTENTS

PREFACE

I started to write this book in my twenties. It was always on my bucket list, like running a marathon. And, well, this labor of love has been quite the ultra-marathon. It's taken me nearly two decades to finish it. It wasn't until I experienced extreme and profound loss in my work and my life that I decided it was time to finish what I started. The option was to go to a therapist or to finish my book. I did both. The finished work is now something very different than what I had planned. It's why I chose the title *Grow with the Flow: Embrace Difference, Overcome Fear, and Progress with Purpose.*

This book is organized around my early adult work and life as a leader, mother, wife, and startup CEO. It's a memoir and shares some of my greatest achievements and blunders and the lessons I've learned along the way. While I've never been one to keep a diary, I have made every effort to check facts wherever possible to provide context around my experiences.

Growth is different for each of us. It has nothing to do with your age. It's my belief that through our experiences, that difference makes us better. Fear stands in our way, but purpose ultimately reigns supreme. Finding that purpose is critical from the moment we are born to the day we close our eyes one last time. I am thankful that I've been able to find my purpose and that I can share these experiences with you with the hopes you will find meaning and purpose in your own work and life.

At the end of this book are some important acknowledgments. Without the friendship and support of so many great people, many of these experiences would not have been possible. I thank everyone who has been a part of this journey and appreciate your grace for any omissions or errors.

Introduction

WE THE PEOPLE

Long ago, our forefathers began the US Constitution with the phrase "We the people." But based on where they were in history and based on the highly visible tilt of all that immediately followed, I think it's fair to say they really meant "We the men" (or, one step further, "We the white men").

Since then, many visionaries have worked to change society's thinking around what "We the people" actually means. Their work always boils down to a fight for equality, a game of widening the lens to better see everyone in the picture. Time and time again, marginalized voices reach the center. The march goes on. The work is hard and the day is long, but the goal is ever within human reach.

This question propels our reaching: What would we (the people) do if we weren't afraid?

Ruth Bader Ginsburg wasn't afraid. She has spent her career fighting in favor of women. She saw a gap, so she hustled like crazy to close it. Her work isn't done yet, but, man, did she yank hard on the edges around that gap. Thank you, Ruth.

Right now, all around the world, women have a conversation going. Although I cannot speak for all of us, I can say that many of us are plain turned off by what our government has turned into. It simply doesn't work. Things don't get done there nowadays.

The conversation both within and emanating from the US government has to change. For a long time, America was a marvel. It's never even been close to perfect, but for decades it delivered decisions based on profound wisdom and a sincere exploration of what it means to be a human being on this earth. Nowadays, it just seems like a shit show.

It's not uncommon for women to avoid political arguments and debates because we've long been told to keep our mouths shut. But lately, I'm seeing a major shift, as women are speaking up both inside of and toward governments around the world. As it turns out, we're not as naturally meek as society has raised us to be. Get ready—we have a colossal number of things we'd like to say. And, like it or not, many of us sense that we can do things better than they're currently being done. Yes, we have a mighty legacy to build upon. But right now, our building powers, rooted in the feminine, are absolutely essential to moving the world forward.

This is not me running for office; the private sector

simply lights me up too much. I see the free market as the place where progress happens at greater speeds and with greater efficiency than within the government. But that doesn't mean I've lost faith in my government, nor does it mean I have no interest in interacting with it.

Quite the contrary—while working on this book, I had the honor of being called to speak in front of Congress. I thought back to when I was five years old, when Ronald Reagan was president. He was my hero at the time; when I saw him on TV, I not only admired him, but I wanted to be him. Or, y'know, at least take over his job. Back then, I wrote Reagan a letter, telling him that my intention was to become the first female president of the United States.

That ambition's long been replaced by other ones. But, man, did getting invited to Congress hit a note for me. I brought my daughter, Ally, along, and let me tell you, something about a woman and her daughter together simply diffuses ideology. I wasn't only a professional woman coming to DC to speak on behalf of the energy community; I was also a proud mom and wife.

When I met with Congress, we discussed the future of energy and what it should look like. Ally fell asleep at some point. She'd been there to support me, but she couldn't help but crash. It didn't matter— from her very presence, I gained strength. I also had the Texas delegation behind me (not literally, but in spirit). I guess they'd looked at me at some point and decided, "That's our girl." No pressure, right?

Our conversation lasted almost five hours, and it was surreal being in that grand hall; some doors down, official business was unfolding relating to Robert Mueller's investigation into President Trump. As I looked around the room, it hit me: Here I am doing what I was once so afraid of. But this is exactly what I was meant to do. Imagine if I'd stayed afraid. Imagine if my comfort zone had won.

Comfort zones around the world are collapsing. The world is shifting in a direction in which we're going to see more winners than we've ever seen before. And I'm not paraphrasing our current president's campaign line about how we're going to win so much that we'll get tired of winning. I'm talking about a seismic shift. I'm seeing a world in which consciousness is ascending. The old paradigms are breaking down—not just in energy or in government, but in the economy, in technology, and in medicine.

For many of us, the current conversation sounds noisy. After all, social media's influence is still a new thing for us to absorb. Humanity's collective psyche is bursting at the edges. We're getting to know each other more than ever. We're facing daily tidal waves of unleashed truth. Can we ride these waves? Can we grow with this flow?

I, for one, will stay here in the water to find out. I'll sometimes get seasick, but most of the time I'll be exhilarated. The world's energy is changing—not just the industrial kind, but the fundamental, spiritual kind too.

Growing with the flow is all about our personal evolution. But here's the thing about personal evolution: it is the primary driver of a little thing called planetary evolution. Each of us is but a puzzle piece. Each of us matters so much. With that in mind, it's our growth that matters most of all.

So go and grow now. Be mighty, be bold, and go and grow.

Chapter One

HURRICANE HARVEY

"Not all storms come to disrupt your
life; some come to clear your path."

—UNKNOWN

We knew the storm was coming. Word was, it would
be an event. Hurricanes, however, are tremendously
unpredictable. We were supposed to brace ourselves,
get ready, and batten down the hatches, but nothing
could have prepared us for what actually happened.

Before the weekend of its arrival, I said to myself,
"Okay, this is just going to be a long, rainy weekend.
Maybe it'll drift into early next week." So I prepared
to put in a couple days of working from home. I lived
in Houston's energy corridor, which is home to many
of the energy companies you're familiar with. It's a
beautiful area, complete with lovely houses, office
spaces, and parks—my own office, also an energy
company, was within biking distance.

My neighborhood and office sit near Buffalo Bayou,
a waterway that flows alongside Terry Hershey Park.

Over the years, we'd seen the bayou take on rain, bubbling and shuddering, but the water never got very high. The waterway, designed to protect Houston, is part of a reservoir system managed by the US Army Corps of Engineers.

I still have the pictures I took of my daughter, Ally, and myself moving some items into an inner room of my office just to be safe. I took all my computer toys with me for the sake of putting in some shifts at home the following week. My husband, Mark, got a good laugh out of this, convinced I was overdoing it, but these storms tend to cause the best and worst situations. In the past, we'd been overprepared, waiting for rain that never came. Other times, stores and gas stations ran out of bread and fuel, and we'd have nothing. With experience, I'd become programmed to veer on the side of caution.

All of this was happening during Ally's first week of school. Just that Monday morning, we'd been snapping pictures outside our house, with no notion of how our lives would be turned upside down in under a week. By Friday, the kids had the day off because of the impending weather.

In due course, all the parents I knew were going crazy. There we were, stuck inside, getting ready for one heck of a long weekend. Some people broke away for trips to the store, only to see key goods such as milk and ice already gone from the shelves. I was among them, venturing out for groceries and to gas up my car. Bread and water were nowhere to be found, and the stations near the freeways were low or out of fuel. I got a haunting chill that I was witnessing an apocalypse.

But Mark and I knew we were literally high and dry, perched nice and safe in a secure area above sea level. While Harvey barreled onto Texas's shores, we marked ourselves "safe" on Facebook. We imagined we'd be the ones helping other people, not the other way around. After all, that's generally how it went when crises came. We were intent on helping Houston through this if things got heavy. As for our own fate, we thought, everything would be fine.

On Saturday, the rain was proving itself to be ambitious. It pounded down without much of a break. One look at our three cars, and we knew there was no way we could drive them out. The streets were draining, but they were filling too.

We knew that, inevitably, the bayous and reservoirs would rise. Though we'd never seen them flood before, that possibility was coming into sharper focus. On TV and on the internet, data charts spelled out the likelihood of flooding based on the elevation of a given street or neighborhood. While keeping an eye on that fun data, I worked with the local moms to set up a WhatsApp channel. That way, we could stay in contact, checking in as to where (if anywhere) we were taking our kids and how we were passing the time or helping others as needs arose.

By midday, Houston was quite a dramatic scene. Still, we were relatively bored. Ally pulled out her savings and counted some money her Paw Paw, my father, had given her. She'd count, "One, two, three . . ." only to soon start the process all over again.

We were just sitting there. Unbeknownst to us, we were sitting ducks.

It was late afternoon Saturday when some quietly alarming news made its way to us. At some point, all the local authorities—the county, the police, and the City of Houston—put out the word that they were inundated. They needed the public to pitch in and help, exactly as expected. No worries, right?

I looked out the window. Sure, water was slicking up the streets, but it was draining. And while the rain kept coming, if it decided to stretch and rest its legs, it didn't do so for more than half a second.

At one point late that afternoon, all we heard was the sound of National Weather Service alerts. They were loud and nonstop. Meanwhile, every screen we looked at—phones, computers, television—reminded us to take cover. It became kind of rhythmic, like those car alarms: Take cover. Take cover. Take cover. By that point, we had taking cover covered. There wasn't anywhere else to go.

And it wasn't just massive amounts of rain we were dealing with. No, that was due to get assistance from some tornadoes. The authorities kept naming subdivisions in their path—nothing near us, but our friends were affected. We'd check in with them to see what was going on. My best friend Jennifer texted me that a tornado wasn't too far from her and her family. They could actually hear it.

Through WhatsApp and Facebook, our own neighborhood sustained some communication and coordination, even though most of us were pinned to one spot. For all the valid criticisms of social media concerning privacy and addiction, without those platforms I would have been (figuratively, though fortunately not literally) in the dark.

Saturday night fell with a fresh downpour of rain. It was like the sky had snapped and was caving in.

"What are we going to do?" I said to Mark.

"Well," he said, "we're going to stay put and ride it out. We have three cars and no way out."

He was right. We'd already been through Hurricanes Ike and Rita, both of which were bad storms in Houston, complete with fuel shortages and road catastrophes. Why would this one be any worse?

Staying put was our sanest option, so we placed our trust in the wisdom of our local authorities.

But staying put was easier said than done. I was ready to jump out of my skin, partly because of the tedium and partly because of a quietly accumulating sense of dread. Something didn't feel right.

And then, as we worked hard to stay put, another alarming rumor drifted onto our radar. According to what I picked up on social media, if the rain didn't back off and take a break, the authorities would have no choice but to release the reservoirs. In other words, the water was so high that there was a risk of the reservoirs overspilling and the dam collapsing. The only way to avert that nightmare was to alleviate some pressure from the reservoirs.

Houston's Mayor Turner quickly shut that down as a rumor. We were told, essentially, to go to sleep.

Some trick that was, as if it were possible to even sleep through this whole ordeal. The sound of rain pounding on the roof and the sides of the house kept me awake, even without factoring in my frayed, coiled nerves. In the meantime, I felt a responsibility to my community. In my own way, I was something of a community leader. My social media presence is ample enough that I feel the need to carefully verify any information I post. As far as that whole reservoir-busting thing, I couldn't see any credible sources behind it, yet it seemed like a real possibility if the rain wouldn't stop. Because I couldn't verify it, I had to go on pretending like I'd never heard it.

But I had.

The apocalypse remained in full swing on Sunday. Alarms kept going off, both in the distance and close by. We also heard Tomahawks overhead, bringing in resources from the Feds.

Looking out at our street, everything seemed . . . fine, actually. That's not to say there wasn't water there, but only up to about mid-calf. With a tall enough car and the needed willpower, someone could certainly get out.

It was about 6:00 p.m. when I saw my neighbors trying to slip out during the littlest lull in the rain. With their three kids in tow, they were heading out on foot. Mark and I gathered near our window, wondering what those guys were doing. As I found out later, they planned to go closer to the highway, away from the back of the nearby park and all the mounting water in the accompanying bayou.

I didn't feel any need to follow their example. I was watching those sewers, which were draining. The lawns looked okay too. Other than the water in the street, along with the accompanying sounds of alarms and helicopters, everything seemed more or less under control.

Until the reservoir rumor came back. I still couldn't fully verify it, but the dang thing was getting traction—both among the public and in my mind. This is not to say it was all I was focused on. Quite the contrary, I found myself turning into a rescue co-ordinator of sorts, finding first responders and iden-tifying some launch points from which people could leave their areas and get into rescue boats. And I was worrying even more about my own home and family.

At 9:00 p.m., Mark and I watched in silence as Jeff Lindner, the local meteorologist for the Harris Council Flood District, delivered news on both tele-vision and social media that brought tears to my eyes. The dams would have to be released due to the pres-sure of rising water. The water in our street was drain-ing, yet the Army Corps of Engineers would have to flood us to save the Houston metropolitan area from a massive catastrophe. Surely, we would get just a few inches of water, and then it would recede.

"Should we start putting some stuff up?" I asked Mark, thinking about taking some of our valuables upstairs.

"Sure," he said. " 'Cause maybe we'll get a few inches."

Lindner was specific: the authorities would begin releasing water at 2:00 a.m. on Monday. We were about four miles from the nearest reservoir, Barker

Dam, but we'd heard that some homes in our neighborhood had already begun taking on water.

My mind launched into motion, trying to figure out how much we personally could be impacted. I looked up probabilities and scenarios online, using gauges for each major intersection in our area. The TV stations were running these too. It was weather prediction on a whole new level.

It didn't take long for the inevitable thought to dawn on me: *We're going to have to get out of here.* Logic had it that if we woke up the next morning (after having not slept, of course) and stepped into water, we could be electrocuted. So, we shut off all the downstairs breakers. It was like a comedy show with no laughter. Mark was asking, "What's this one? What's this one?"

We also stacked our furniture. Although things were tense, we were still thinking about the water in terms of inches. Nobody within earshot was talking in terms of feet—although they should have been.

Exactly one year earlier, Mark had been in the process of losing his mother, Mary Ann. We were counting our blessings she wasn't there to struggle through this with us. Meanwhile, a more practical issue crossed our minds: For some reason, we'd never bought flood insurance. I was always of the mind that you should have plenty more than you need in the event of a (literally) rainy day. But to be fair, we didn't live in an area that required it, and 85 percent of our neighborhood didn't have it. The realization that we weren't insured brought us to our knees. Mark was visibly upset, but "We'll fix this," he told me.

I couldn't see how. I was devoting too much mental bandwidth to anticipating what was to come, much less pondering if or when it would be fixed. I was panicked. I was upset. I was scared. Leaving my home would likely mean a boat rescue, and I wasn't having it.

After we'd prepared the first floor of our home, we went upstairs to "sleep." Because we'd turned off the condensing unit downstairs, the AC was out. It was getting hot, but that was the least of our worries.

We still had TV and power. I was still on WhatsApp. We were trading pictures, stories, and prayers. We were getting acquainted with the whos, whats, wheres, and whens of the emergency in progress.

Later, we learned that the government had started releasing reservoir water as early as 8:00 or 9:00 p.m. on Sunday. By midnight, my yard was filled with bayou water. But the big landmark release point, as far as the official word went, was still 2:00 a.m. Monday.

The next morning, I went to the window in Ally's bedroom. As promised, there was water. Outside was essentially *Waterworld*. I saw people's furniture floating out of their yards—lawn furniture from the area, but also interior pieces that the water must've carried our way from more impacted areas. I saw a car stuck in the street—literally in the middle of the street—just stranded there. Up and down the neighborhood, people's cars were taking on water. People's mailboxes were submerged too. The most noteworthy thing about this water was that it wasn't just sitting there. It had a current. It had *force*.

The good news was that I could still see our lawn. "Let's walk the greens," I said to Mark. My plan was to reach the high point in the middle of the street, from which we could get out.

When we got outside, the water came up just below my knee. Its current showed no sign of relenting. I looked at Mark, who had Ally perched on his shoulders. We left our dog, Maddie, behind so we could leave first, and she was scared out of her mind. All our thoughts were focused on that high point up the street. Get there. Get out. It was that simple.

And yet we stood there. Before we knew it, we were back inside, watching the window. I texted people to find out what they were doing, how—and if—they were escaping.

Then it happened. I didn't even give it much

thought; it just seemed like the practical thing to do. I put the word out publicly on Facebook that we needed a boat.

From where we waited upstairs, it was surreal to hear a knock on the door. That sound had once been the most natural thing in the world. Now, it was like something out of a dream.

I went downstairs and opened the door. Before me stood a Hispanic gentleman who barely spoke English. Essentially, he said to me, "Boat. Take you. Safe."

Mark insisted we leave. His plan was to stay back and gather some things. When Ally heard this, she screamed, "Daddy! Come with us!" But he didn't budge. Mark also asked (read: told) me to take off my wedding ring. For some reason, we were worried about losing it. Kind of a strange reason for me to take it off my finger, but that's more or less the wavelength we were operating on.

I pressed it into his hand, telling him to put it somewhere safe, so he said he'd put it upstairs in Ally's room. Then he planned to put together a bag—laptops, clothes, other essentials—and come on foot to meet us.

I didn't let him go without a fight. We argued as the man with the boat looked on. Ally kept screaming her head off. Maddie had no idea what to think.

Then Mark said, "Just go." So we turned around.

There was the boat, floating in the water. When we drifted away, I turned to look at Mark and Maddie. *How is this me? How has my life turned into this?* I thought.

In general, there wasn't much room for thinking. I was trying to be strong for Ally. "Baby, it's okay," I said to her. "Mommy's here. We're going to get safe."

One thing I did take with me was my cell phone, which I'd been fortunate to charge completely overnight. I took a picture of the man in the little boat. I took a picture of our house as it receded, taking on so much water.

Sometimes, I look back at these pictures. Strangely, that one of our house from the boat had a detail in it I hadn't noticed while taking it. It was in the background, yet pretty much unmissable: an American flag, and just beyond that, a WaveRunner.

The man with the boat got us to safety. When we stepped on land, the revelation hit me like a jolt of electricity: I had no place to go, and I had no car. All I had were my daughter and the clothes on my back. For a split second, I asked myself, *Is this what homelessness feels like?*

I'm sure, of course, what I was going through paled in comparison to the real thing. But that moment flattened me. I was in shock. I had no money on me and no place for us to sleep. For the first time in my adult life, I felt lost, isolated, and completely out of control.

Word got out about a meetup point. My neighbors who'd driven out the night before had some family in a safe spot with a house. That was our destination.

Ally clung to me, all fifty pounds of her, neither loosening her grip nor letting go. I knew the meetup point was only two streets over, but I was completely turned around; I had no clue how to find it. Thank God for my phone, which routed me there via GPS.

All the while, I was pelted with piercing rain—and texts from my network:

"Did you get out?"

"Where r u?"

"Are u okay?"

Finally, we got settled at the meetup point, a house owned by the Fitzjarrald family. At the moment, mercifully, they were my family's only tie to civilization. But I still had only half a family. It took an hour and a half for Mark to show up, with Maddie on a leash.

One thing worth noting about a crisis: While it's unfolding, you're not necessarily doing your clearest thinking, much less making your wisest decisions. It's eerie how things that make sense in the moment—like me taking off my wedding ring—show deteriorating logic in retrospect. Add a total lack of sleep to the equation, and we ended up doing some flat-out crazy things.

For example, that night, Mark took Maddie back home. He put her in an upstairs bathroom with food and water and locked the door. We didn't want to be a burden on anybody, and Maddie's presence was a degree too unstable. Taking her back to our water-threatened house wasn't much of a solution, but at the time, it made sense.

While Mark had been trying to figure out what to do with Maddie, I got a call from my lawyer, Marianne. "Let me come get you guys," she said. Ally and I ended up spending Monday night at Marianne's, but by the time Mark got back out of our neighborhood, he ended up sleeping at the Fitzjarralds'.

By now, the city was without power. Whereas our power had hung in there during the worst of the storm, the city had decided to cut it entirely. With so many families caught in their homes, the risk of electric shock was just too high.

The next morning, Tuesday, Mark returned home in chest-high water to get Maddie. As she swam out, her nerves were beyond frazzled. Mark also saw that we had lost our three cars, which meant a trip to the car rental service was now in order. When I got there, I learned their new, improvised policy: If we weren't Toyota customers, we could not rent from that location. So elderly people—including my seventy-five-year-old neighbors—were being given the choice to either go somewhere else or buy a brand-new car.

"These rentals are for our customers only," the manager kept repeating. The Enterprise rental guy tried to reason with the boss, but he wasn't having it. He saw a fresh new revenue stream, and he wasn't about to let it go. So, I pretty much threw a fit, telling him exactly what I thought of his new policy. Eventually, he budged, we got a car, and I was able to help my neighbors too.

I didn't even know how much I needed to preserve all the energy I could.

Marianne had taken in several evacuee families, ours included. Things were so upside down, with Mark going back and forth between what was left of our house and our temporary residences, that at one point Ally and I spent two nights with the Fitzjarralds without him.

During that time, Ally thought I'd left Mark and Maddie at our flooded house. She'd be off having fun with the other kids, playing and running, but when it came to having anything to do with me—forget it. I was on her pay-no-mind list.

Finally, as I'd been promising her, Mark showed up for good. I fell right into his arms. "I'm glad I'm here," he said. It was beginning to hit me that this was the scariest thing I'd ever dealt with.

> **For the first time in our lives, we understood what it was like to go unseen. I also felt an unfamiliar sadness. We were always the ones to help and not the ones to take help. As the help poured in, it was difficult to accept.**

The next couple days were a blur of activities that, while ordinary on the surface, were charged with deep sadness and desperation. Mark, an executive attorney for an energy company, kept running over to work to address the company's recovery of people and assets. While I was shuttling back and forth to work too, I was also filing for FEMA aid, along with any other form of aid that crossed my mind. We had one foot in civilization, and the other firmly in the dark ages.

I also kept trying to rally attention in the direction

of our neighborhood. Due to our affluent community's relative stability, the authorities left us to our own devices. Their attitude was almost as though our neighborhood had bounced back and was open for business. The local authorities told the national news we were fine. But I told anyone who would listen that we were far from open; we were submerged in water.

Everybody in our neighborhood had one major asset to speak of: their home. As such, all of us had been robbed of whatever wealth we had. There were plenty of people who never got out. Elderly people passed away. People drowned. People succumbed to heart attacks. People were electrocuted. For the first time in our lives, we understood what it was like to go unseen. We also felt an unfamiliar sadness. We were always the ones to help and not the ones to take help. As the help poured in, it was difficult to accept.

Rescue and recovery boats blanketed the city's west side. Launch locations, where the water was deep enough for people to get pushed out on boats, were established. As for the Red Cross—forget it; they were too inundated to respond. The storm, of course, hadn't discriminated in terms of socioeconomic status. More and more, I witnessed that there's no middle class in today's America. The dividing line is clear—either you're rich or poor. Our neighborhood had working young families and retirees, but by today's standards, we were living in luxury.

For a time, the name of the game was supplies. How could we get supplies into our neighborhood? A few miles from home, our neighborhood women's group mobilized to send over water and other key goods. The group set up an Amazon registry, from which good Samaritans could route deliveries to our area. It was all about getting the neighborhood back. Anything that couldn't be used, we sent to an area west of us that had been devastated by water.

I got used to not knowing what day it was, nor the time of day. I do know it took twelve days for our mayor to pay our street a visit, and when he did, he was greeted by no small amount of anger. I'd never seen more people in need. Poor people, people of means—it didn't matter. At that time, we were all just people, trying to get back on our feet.

Before long, the inevitable moment arrived: It was time to gut our house. An army of church and civic groups flowed into town, and they got right to work. Around that time, my father was attempting to travel into Houston, though he didn't know how. Many routes were blocked off due to water. In any case, he was determined, and as he had throughout my life, he came through for me. Dad was there when our house was gutted; he actually helped with it. There he was, my seventy-something father jackhammering tile with my friends Jen and Cathy.

Of all the tough things I've experienced, nothing

comes close to losing my house. Sure, people like to say it's just a structure—an object—but that's not true. It was my memories. It was my sanctuary. It was the things I'd picked out, the things I'd earned the right to own. It was something I thought I'd earned the right to, taken away from me by a rush of water.

In time, I became used to traveling by boat. I'd tried toughing it out and walking in that filthy water, but it gave me a staph infection. It's one thing to deal with an infection, but another thing entirely to do so while semi-homeless.

We stayed at Marianne's for at least a week. After that, we spent two weeks with our friends Jen and Chris. Soon our goal was to get an apartment. This meant credit checks, which meant accessing information we'd either lost or boxed away. Many people initially migrated to hotels because it's FEMA practice to place them there. But my mind wasn't on hotels; I was looking for areas where properties hadn't flooded, because like every other "resource," the government was inundated. I was also wondering how long a lease we should be looking at. In other words: When, if ever, will this nightmare finally end?

We found a place nearby, close to our house and Ally's school. To prepare us for our move into the apartment, my best girlfriends went to Bed, Bath & Beyond and texted me about what color towels I wanted. I was like, "I don't care. Just get 'em." I also asked for the cheapest furniture set, saying I'd pay them back. Linens. Utensils. Beds. We needed it all.

With each new day, I learned more about where my relationships stood with the people in my life. My tribe came to my side. My friends, extended family, neighbors, and community rallied behind the Mehnerts. Welcoming us to our new apartment, people showed up with meals and even gift cards. Never had I seen more people coming together and giving so selflessly.

Many others were helpful too. I heard the words "What can I do for you?" as regularly as "Hello" and "Goodbye." It was always hard to answer that question, though. I mean, how does one replace absolutely everything?

Like everyone else, just one year prior, I'd seen the 2016 US presidential election unfold. I'd watched our whole world at odds as people subjected each other to merciless and vicious stereotypes. Yet there on the ground level, after Hurricane Harvey, I came to see that people were just as human as they'd always been.

Another revelation hit me—one more personal, and thus more forceful: If my growing business were to fail in the aftermath of the storm, I would be 100 percent fine with that. This feeling was uncharacteristic of me. My whole adult life had been devoted to striving, achieving, and overcoming. Now, failure was on the table, and that was fine. I mean, nobody could have blamed me, right? If my business went under, it would have been Mother Nature's fault, not mine, so the optics would have been okay.

But it wasn't just a superficial assessment. I too would have been okay. Reality had humbled me to a point beyond caring about succeeding. Surviving, for now, was enough.

> **Nobody can force us to be ready to move forward. We alone know when we're ready to grow. But sometimes, for better or for worse, life goes ahead and makes us ready.**

And then the most beautiful thing happened. Day by day, I came to realize that the community I'd built in the course of creating my business was showing up when I needed it to. I'd wanted these people to help each other, but now their priority was to help me. And as I saw that karmic circle close, I realized I absolutely could not give up on that community.

As for my business, well . . . it soared. I wish I could explain how this tragedy, which tested me and brought me to the brink, paved the way for my business to reach its current explosive conditions. It's not like I suddenly became superhuman. I'm not like the women you hear about who, when their children are trapped under a car, suddenly get a rush of adrenaline and lift the car up off the ground.

Quite the contrary, I've been exhausted. Whenever I hear a raindrop, I get a burst of post-traumatic stress. And ever since the storm, I've felt like I've been scrambling, hustling, improvising—just trying to make things work. Somehow, things are working better than ever.

I've come to call this process Growing with the Flow. "Flow" represents the water that rushed into my life. I've become humbler. I've learned how to ask for things: help, support, understanding, even a listening ear. Every day, I learn more, still.

This book is about Growing with the Flow. It's about the fact that nobody can force us to make a step. Nobody can force us to be ready to move forward. We alone know when we're ready to grow.

But sometimes, for better or for worse, life goes ahead and makes us ready. When that happens, we have no choice but to flow. The alternatives are to ignore the current or to fight back against it, both of which likely mean certain death.

When the current takes you, you have to grow where it leads. In my case, it's led to deeper humility,

sharper reality, and a greater sense of what's important. All such things are forms of abundance, ones that
have reflected in my business's astonishing growth
and my desire to live a simpler life.

All my life, I've been interested in connecting people. Connected people, I believe, are always safer and
happier. This book is the next step in my lifelong
journey of deep and meaningful community connections, and the experiences that I created or that
have been thrust upon me. When the community
I helped came back to help me, I realized the cycle
wasn't complete. I knew it was time to step it up a
notch, to help at a higher level. Not only will helping
you help me, it will—I sincerely believe—help the
whole world.

Not all storms come to disrupt your life; some
come to clear your path. With the utmost humility, I
offer these pages to you.

Chapter Two

READY FOR TAKEOFF

"The world is your oyster.
Go harvest your pearl."

—HENRY LANCE WALTHALL

My dad was always big on self-reliance when I was growing up. At seventy-six, he still is. As the father of three daughters, he steeled us for the world that awaited us, frequently harping on the values of independence. He often repeated that we should never marry a man just for his money.

"The world is your oyster," he'd say. I heard that from him as a child, and I still hear it as an adult. I can do anything I want, be anything I want.

After college, I went to St. Louis, Missouri. I could go into all the reasons, or I could just give you the simple version: I followed a boy. He was my college sweetheart (note: not my future husband). I wonder if my dad was unsettled by that. He must have been like, *"Hmm, did Katie somehow miss the last, I don't know, three hundred memos I sent her?"*

In any case, when I followed that boy, I did it as though it were my place. Like that was what a girl did after finishing school. It didn't help that my first job after college laid me off.

I remember not wanting to call my dad after that one. I'd spent a year in that job, bringing in no money. In fact, maybe there was some creepy omen at play, because my last paycheck was literally $666.66. So much for the world being my oyster.

After playing a little game of avoidance, I finally called home. I did not want to ask my dad for money. "Don't ask him for money, don't ask him for money, don't—" repeated like a mantra in my head. After all, he'd always drilled into me the idea that I should never expect handouts from people, even if they loved me. Accordingly, I've long been the type to save for rainy days (or hurricane-y days, as the case turned out to be).

Shortly into our call, my dad said, "Am I going to write you a check and send you some money?" I hadn't even asked. I hadn't even wanted it, due to all the things he'd told me. But his general message was: "I'm your dad, and I'm here for you when you need it."

Naturally, I took the money—I needed to pay my bills—but taking it felt lousy. Even though my dad was sending me mixed messages, contradicting his longstanding lessons about self-reliance with a sudden show of charity, I had by then internalized his value of independence. I wasn't relieved by him popping up an unknown emergency exit. Guilt chewed me up.

But it was okay because his tough side made the more lasting impression. He'd grown up working-class. His whole life narrative was studded with stories about working his ass off. And rightfully so—he worked hard, went to college, and became successful. Accordingly, taking his money didn't mean just benefitting from his resources—it was benefitting from his sweat. I felt the difference.

Meanwhile, when I'd gone to St. Louis, my dad's mentality had been that if I wanted that path, I was going to pay for it—literally. I remember pitching the whole journey to him in this endless, elaborate spiel of all the reasons I should go, all the pros, all the reasons he should have faith in me and my decision. Just imagine if it hadn't been the 1990s and I'd had access to PowerPoint. When I was finally done, he said, "You put a lot of effort into this." He looked at me with a charge in his eyes. I had impressed him! But in addition to acknowledging my effort, he also gave me a practical notice: "The National Bank of Dad is closed," he said.

So when it came time to go back to the bank, and to mercifully find its doors wide open, I was rather reluctant to step inside. Things could have gone two ways. It's the classic liberal-conservative argument: Is the government better off being your loving guardian or your rugged provider of freedom? My dad certainly had both impulses within him, but the rugged parts sunk deeper into my system.

Not only is my dad an advocate for independence, but he is a big believer in working for what you want in life. And not just working for it, but working your ass off for it. Not only being immune to handouts, but being proud of whatever you built because you had to do it by yourself.

When I built Pink Petro, it was every bit a labor of crazy love. Every step along the way, the process was guided by my will to carve out my own piece of territory on this earth. But that's not to say every detail of its founding was carefully and meticulously planned. No, a degree of spontaneity was involved.

The year was 2013. If I can attribute my success to anything, it's the fact that I saw gaps, I saw them early, and I was able to connect and close them. That's how I built what I built, and why it became bigger than me.

In fact, I should go a little easy on the spontaneity factor, because it wasn't as though the idea for Pink Petro and Experience Energy were nowhere in my consciousness and then popped aboard from the vast emptiness of the cosmos.

Instead, a trio of unique factors had been stirring in my mind: 1) I was picking up the sense that people had an appetite for new ways to connect. Social media reflected this. People were becoming open to forms of emotional connection linked with technology, which had never existed before.

2) I had a conjoining awareness that as people's ideas and forms of connection shift, markets shift with them. It all comes down to basic human behavior: where there are humans, there are markets. Accordingly, as humans forge new ways of relating, markets will inevitably crop up within those brand-new forums. And before they crop up, there is the opportunity to be the one who furnishes the markets.

Meanwhile, the energy sector, where I already worked before starting Pink Petro, was in a state of crisis, trying to get back on its feet in the wake of a price crash and increasing social cries about climate change. But in its rawest form, the chaotic energy emanating from the crisis was also vital, positive life energy. In other words, people were on the move. They might not have been able to see the future, but they were certainly scrambling to get there.

I, however, was seeing flashes of what the future might offer. People's appetite for new forms of connection + the energy sector in crisis + the underlying potential for a new market = the embryo of something different. But what, exactly?

Well, let's not forget 3) the women's movement. Mind you, this was well before #MeToo gained momentum in 2017. Still, consciousness was changing around women, LGBTQ people, and people of color. They were finally getting a seat at the table, being listened to, considered, and represented in the cultural conversation. I saw it online, and I saw it at the office. The numbers were still horrific, but the socialization for change was becoming big.

> **You open worlds (and minds) by making them more social. If a given sphere is not open, it's probably not friendly. It needs the sunlight of socialization pumped into it. And I'd long had this sneaking suspicion that I was in a reasonable position to bring in the light.**

Interestingly, the forward push to empower women unfolded with simultaneous pushback from bullies and assholes. That's always how the pendulum swings: as one marginalized group gains power, the ones who've always had the power have to edit their presumptions about how power remains intact. This trade-off comes into play around anti-harassment, anti-racism, anti-homophobia—pretty much anything that's anti-being-an-asshole.

For so long in business, the presumption was that one had to be an asshole to get ahead. Not only was this proving false, but it was also getting run over by sheer moral understanding. In other words, we knew being a bully and being successful didn't have to go hand in hand, and we knew being an authentic person and being successful was a more natural and powerful combination.

Let's not play any games of denial around this: Some people who run big companies (and even small ones) are outright demonic. They've been rewarded for behaving like sociopaths. Equality doesn't factor into their worldview, let alone their world. It's their world; we're just living in it.

But people have been waking up to the fact that this is a problem. Immoral behavior has led to the wrong people accruing too much power, and as a result, society has lost many opportunities for gaining equality.

Enter social media. Suddenly, new voices are in the cultural conversation. Not only are they being heard, but they can't be turned off—which means they can no longer be ignored. Now the playing field is leveling, and in some cases creating serious division.

Of course, change toward equality doesn't simply come about when we speak up. I was in an industry notorious for its closed-mindedness around equality. I found myself asking, How do you open an industry that's so closed-minded? How do you open a world that's so closed-minded? The two things live on a married index.

The answer was simple: You open worlds (and minds) by making them more social. You create conversations. If a given sphere is not open, it's probably not friendly. It needs the sunlight of socialization pumped into it. And I'd long had this sneaking suspicion that I was in a reasonable position to bring in the light.

One particular event steered me toward that light in 2013, when I was headed to London for a trip. I was a safety executive for BP post–oil spill, on my way to make a presentation to the C-suite leaders with my boss and our team. The flight to London turned out to be less important than the one home, but it was still a pivotal event. As we departed America, I was reading a book I'd heard a lot of hype about: *Lean In: Women, Work, and the Will to Lead* by Facebook COO Sheryl Sandberg.

Something I miss about being on planes all the time (which is not to say I miss being on planes in general) is having the chance to read for long stretches of time. Nowadays, that's a rare commodity, so I relished it on this flight. And—no surprise here—I dug the book. I didn't agree with everything Sheryl had to say, but her book deserved its hype.

In fact, one question she posed struck a chord with me: What would you do if you weren't afraid? Fear is what most often holds us back. Circumstances definitely play a role in building a wall between us and our dreams, but fear tends to be the biggest barrier. Fear is what makes us dish out excuses, reminding us we're limited because of this and that.

This passage hit me like a lightning bolt, but the rest of the book could not have been more timely— not just to the global conversation, but to my own life's particulars. It was all about taking a seat at the table. It wasn't for everybody; some reviews roundly slammed Sheryl for the inevitable limitations of her perspective. But as part of her target audience, to me *Lean In* was instantly a keeper.

Except that I missed its message. Or I didn't get it right away. No, for that to happen, the universe would have to intervene.

At that point in my life, I was comfortable. I was an executive with an awesome career in energy. So even though "What would you do if you weren't afraid?"

spoke to me, I didn't consciously feel afraid. This is a delicate matter because comfort has a deep, intrinsic relationship to fear. There's being comfortable, and then there's being in your comfort zone. So much of life comes down to figuring out which is which.

Being comfortable isn't bad. We crave comfort, and when we finally attain it, it's generally fleeting. But, hey, maybe we needed to feel grounded and safe for a while. We spend our lives battling challenges, so if you manage to grab a piece of comfort, more power to you.

Comfort isn't a problem until it becomes the endgame. At that point, mere comfort makes way for comfort zones, where people go to die (not to grow). Maybe those around us see us limiting ourselves, but we are too afraid to change the game up.

I was in that state then. Wanting to make a difference, in 2012, I'd just left a global career at Shell for BP after the 2010 Deepwater Horizon oil spill. It had been a huge leap: big leadership role, bigger impact, bigger paycheck. In its aftermath, I felt myself constantly exhaling, like, Whew! I wasn't really feeling charged for another fight, but ready or not, I was on my way to London.

I landed on a Monday, Sheryl's manifesto fresh in my mind. I had my professional dial cranked up to maximum. I was giving it my all.

Until I ate an unfortunate piece of cheese. Call it

food poisoning. Call it an allergy attack. Whatever it was, once it hit my system, my trip to London became a trek through hell. There's no sickness quite as disorienting as one that occurs when traveling. None of my dependable resources, in terms of people or places, are readily at hand. Sure, I had good colleagues around me, but they weren't my family or my doctors. Add to this the backdrop of a foreign country—the rhythms, vibes, nuances, and accents—and I felt like I'd been dropped in *Alice in Wonderland*. Only instead, I was holed up in my hotel room. It was a classy environment, but there I was at the center of it, my lymph system working to wrench out a dragon of a disease.

My boss, BP lifetimer and all-around great guy Dave Redeker, was there. His team was populated entirely by women; he was ahead of the curve. He couldn't have been more attentive, checking in on me and making sure the hotel staff tended to me with Sprite and saltines.

Sprite and saltines, though, weren't about to cut it. In retrospect, cheese be damned, I think I was in the throes of a bodily protest. My very being—physical and spiritual—was screaming out at me. When Sheryl's book hadn't set off loud enough alarm bells, the universe had ushered in a backup plan. And there it was, right in my face and in my guts, wailing like there was no such thing as tomorrow.

I thought about going to the hospital, but I wasn't too trusting of the UK's medical system. So I toughed it out, even though I was a freaking mess. My thoughts weren't operating in their normal trustworthy manner, but somehow I came around to thinking that even though I wasn't yet 100 percent well, I was well enough to drag myself onto an airplane and fly home. The thought was daunting—heck, the thought of walking across the room was daunting—but I figured I could scale the wall of each passing second and make it through.

All the while, I kept thinking, to the extent that I could think at all, *Why am I so sick? Why do I feel so uneasy?* Much later, I found the answer: my body was responding to Sheryl's question. It was as though I needed to release the sludge, the habits, the comfort that had been my former self to make way for a new me, someone I certainly had not anticipated being. There she was, charging at me. Who was this woman?

I thought the BP job was what I had wanted; it was supposed to be my dream job. I was enacting sweeping safety standards and influencing cultural change. I was showing up every day to add safety, sanity, responsibility, consciousness, and strength to an industry that needed, and still needs, all of the above.

That swanky London hotel room reflected all the luxury the job's nature implied, so why was I so at odds with my surroundings? Why, instead of being at one with the room, had I turned into a pale, sweaty monster, crawling on my belly into the bathroom?

Those who travel internationally for work know the deal when it's time to fly home: you roll out of bed, hit the airport, and get on a plane. Under ordinary circumstances, it's a little stressful. Under my circumstances, I couldn't believe I was even standing, let alone walking. And unlike the rest of my team, I hadn't switched to the airport hotel. No, I had been clinging by my fingernails to the other one, further away.

When my team had left, eyeing me as though they might never see me again, I reassured them, "No worries. I'm gonna water it up." Water and Sprite were the mainstays of my diet, mixed with some British biscuits to keep my stomach from caving in. When I boarded the plane home, water was the only thing sloshing around in my stomach.

But as the flight boarded, I suddenly had a craving for wine. I was going from a tolerance of only water and soda to a mind that was saying, "Sure, Katie, you can go for a little wine right now." The thought did not materialize out of fear. I wasn't fortifying myself against a long, scary flight. Mere hours prior, the very thought of wine would have made me hurl, but when the flight attendant brought some over, I felt tranquil. Centered, even. And I was feeling brave enough to mentally revisit Sheryl's question: What would you do if you weren't afraid?

I can't even say this visitation was intentional; the question had burrowed itself into my subconscious. It appealed to my natural will to push forward and grow. Because when you frame your life in terms of what you're afraid of, you're treated to a nice, hard look at your boundaries.

Apparently, the universe wasn't shrieking loud enough for me yet. I was in for yet another hard kick in the pants. Fortunately, the next one didn't arrive in the form of a gut-wrenching illness. It came in the form of the person seated next to me . . . and was a very good reason for me requesting a glass of wine.

I'd long been used to traveling solo, an activity that for some reason involves being asked a lot of questions, generally by men. I could be flying in business class, then get upgraded to first class and think I was in for some relaxation—until the "gentleman" beside me started pelting me with questions: "You're all by yourself? Where's your husband?" As if I need a keeper to get from point A to point B.

This particular flight, on which I was sitting next to a random guy, was no different. Although I suppose "random" might be unfair because our conversation helped redirect the course of my life. I don't recall the dude's real name, so we'll call him Bubba. If you had seen him, you would agree it's fitting. For starters, he had this hard liquor thing going on, probably bourbon. He'd had a lot of it, and he was swirling a glass when I'd sat down.

We started talking, and he asked what I do for a living. When I told him, he swerved wildly into a pause. Then he asked, inevitably, "Where is your husband?"

"At home," I said.

"Where is your daughter?" he asked by way of a follow-up, apparently not getting the message. Unrelenting, he soon asked what he'd clearly been thinking the whole time: "Why are you not at home?"

I wanted to check my calendar to confirm it was 2013. The question about my husband was commonplace. The daughter follow-up was pushing it. But the last question? This guy was giving away all those other guys' secrets. This is not to say all men who follow this line of questioning are necessarily evil. People generally make assumptions too easily. In my situation, people commonly assume I'm trailing my husband financially, and that he should be the one traveling for business. Or he should have at least joined me, lest I be swallowed up by the big, scary world.

But these encounters with inquisitive men tend to occur in first class, where I am often the only woman seated there. Flying first class is a great example of how sexism intersects with classism. These guys were shelling out major cash for their tickets, ostensibly to fly in comfort. But on some deep level, did flying comfortably mean flying without women? Regardless of the reason, powerful men constitute something of a club. They're certain of their right to be there. As such, when a woman walks among their ranks, she's in danger of being questioned like a common gate-crasher.

On that trip in 2013, I explained to Bubba that my husband was at home, watching our three-year-old daughter. My husband is an ass-kicking business success story in his own right, and it's sad that I feel the need to defend that, as though being a good father at home isn't something to be proud of. But I digress.

Later in our dull conversation, Bubba issued the final kicker. In his mind, he was just a drunk charmer. In reality, he was about to alter the face of the energy business because he had the nerve to ask, "What's a pretty young lady like you doing in a dark, dangerous business like oil?"

The light bulb that went off above my head was so bright, it could have blinded the pilot and crashed us into the Atlantic Ocean. In a split second, I said to myself, *I am going to fix this.*

Year in and year out, I'd heard many comments that there aren't enough women in the energy sector. Sure, I certainly saw women, but I agreed they were in short supply. Sometimes I was the only one present, and when I wasn't, it was generally behind office walls rather than in the "dark, dangerous" field.

Not only did I intend to fix the representation issue, but I wanted to simultaneously fix this "dark and dangerous" perception. Obviously, the two were interrelated, almost as though the field were brutish and manly so as to keep women away.

> **The light bulb that went off above my head was so bright, it could have blinded the pilot and crashed us into the Atlantic Ocean. In a split second, I said to myself, *I am going to fix this.***

Without a doubt, the industry I work in is risky. We handle hydrocarbons. We encounter daunting technical scenarios. We're involved with steel and pumps and heat and fire and chemicals. All of this is very serious and intrinsically masculine. Yet there's a more radical way of looking at it: natural resources are a gift from Mother Earth.

Before you paint me as some crazed anti-environmentalist, let me frame this in a broader context. People look at the oil industry and think "climate change." That conscious connection is the result of the hard and diligent work of many people who are concerned about our planet's welfare. Yet while environmentalists express dismay over how slowly we're transitioning to newer, more sustainable forms of energy, they overlook the very reason for that slowness, namely that oil is responsible for much of our basic modern comfort. From our cars to our plastics to our pacemakers, we're dependent on oil in ways that improve our lives. I'm talking about the fundamental building blocks of civilization. Can energy be improved? Of course, it has to be. Remember: I'm a hurricane survivor. I know what a bad mood Mother Earth is in.

But I also can't deny that Earth is providing us a great deal through the energy she lets us use. As such, the industry in which I work is just as feminine as it is masculine, even if that femininity often goes unseen. My industry provides, nurtures, promotes, and sustains life. Yes, the snake is now eating its own tail. The energy I'm praising has revealed its latent dark side. But it's possible to acknowledge that dark side at the same time as its overwhelming goodness. I feel protective of that goodness in a way that I daresay only a woman can.

I wanted desperately to bring Bubba up to speed on a concept that would have blown his mind: a woman is capable of doing a job traditionally thought of as a man's—and vice versa (high-five to hubby, home with the kid). My father had taught me that it was okay to speak up to an older gentleman, but this guy was so old that he'd probably flipped his white wig when he saw me wandering around outside a kitchen. So I steeled myself to drink my wine instead.

Fortunately, things didn't get heated. We still hadn't taken off yet, and before I knew it, the flight attendant was hovering over us to let us know about a safety issue. "We have a small problem," she said. "We may have to deplane everybody and move to a different plane." The gods had managed to save me from this awful man.

I asked the flight attendant to reseat me, and I was happy to take coach. In other words, flying first class next to Bubba was not flying first class. I wanted to be as far away from him as possible. Unfortunately, the flight was full, so I suggested that I trade seats with a random person. Everybody craves first class, right? She wasn't having it, though. In lieu of a new seat, she offered me water.

Due to the safety issue, our devices had to remain off. I was trapped next to Bubba sans technology, but the two things kind of went together, seeing as Bubba was mentally in the Stone Age. That's when I had my cocktail napkin moment. Bubba and I had stopped talking, so I started spilling my mind onto those napkins. I was exhausted, but not past the point of caring. I sketched out notes: How could I change the perception of our industry? How could I accelerate the progress of women? How could I accelerate the progress and understanding of what we do and get more engaged with it? How could I get people in my own industry rallied behind the fact that we desperately needed to transition to new fuels? How can equality + environment = new economy?

My pen had trouble keeping up with my mind. My mind had trouble keeping up with my pen. Thanks to Bubba, my father, bare luck, and Mother Earth, I was a woman on fire.

It's like this: You have to look for the gaps. "Ordinary" people (there's really no such thing) tend to see what's there. Extraordinary people see what's not there and find a way to provide it.

In a way, this goes back to how I was raised. My dad didn't want me to perceive any net beneath me. He hoped to nurture my self-reliance. Part of being self-reliant is being resourceful—or being able to claim the future as something you can control and influence, and act accordingly. A big part of this comes down to filling gaps. The future itself is a gap—it's not here yet, but day by day, we occupy it. We turn the unknown into the known. If you want an ordinary life, you can do what's safe and predictable, and stick to the well-worn pathways. But, man, it gets wild when you branch off onto the ones that were never there before.

It happened fast. After socializing the idea, my first client, Cindy Patman, an HR executive and colleague at Halliburton, wrote me a gorgeous five-figure check, fully aware that I hadn't created anything yet. All I had were my cocktail napkins and a great big gap. Her check was a way of saying, "Close it."

One day, likewise, the local media called me. They asked, "What's Pink Petro? We heard you're launching it." Those were the reporter's exact words. And that was the moment I realized it was real.

"Look," I said, "can you give me two days?" I was on the line at that point. All the people around me not only got what I was doing, but dug it to the extreme. The message I kept getting was, "Oh, my God, Katie, this is so you. This is perfect. Go, go, go!" So I started a website and a social media channel. I was officially in beta-testing mode (whatever that means).

And then, as ready as I could be at that time, I called the reporter back for that interview. And I faked my way through the entire conversation. But one fact I offered in it turned out to be real. I told the reporter, riffing off the top of my head, that Pink Petro was set to launch in the first quarter of the following year, March 8, 2015, on International Women's Day.

I'd never told anyone this before. I wasn't even aware of it myself. Yet it came out of my mouth, so that was the goal I stuck to. It had become real—the thing had taken on life. Pink Petro and Experience Energy were born, moving at their own paces, following their own minds, and using me kind of like a puppet. And closing every gap in sight.

Chapter Three

KNOW YOUR MEANING

"The lessons we learn, of course, derive
from experiences which were had in a
certain time and in a certain place."

—LORD JOHN BROWNE

Those of us who were around at the turn of the century remember Y2K, when we were expecting our computers to crash right at the start of the year 2000. Needless to say, that never happened. Later, in 2001, the 9/11 terrorist attacks delivered the level of chaos people had been anticipating, albeit in a different way. I, meanwhile, was experiencing a chaos all my own.

In late 2000, I moved to Houston. I had just left a long-term relationship, and I'd been laid off from my marketing job in St. Louis. Afterward, I found myself venturing into the world of start-ups. Right around Y2K, a company in Houston named Enron called me to say, "Hey, we would really love you to come here and get into the energy business." Back then, people wanted a piece of that beloved company.

One of the many things my father always told me was to never, ever get into the energy business. Of course, that's exactly what I did. Enron then wasn't the Enron we know now, forever marked by its corruptness. At the time, though, you should have seen its stock offers. Everyone not only knew Enron, but they knew Enron was the best thing going. This was a brand of Kool-Aid no one could resist. I was eager to get aboard, and I was looking at a sizable increase in pay. It was a new time, a new chapter, a new world.

Six months into it, I got sick.

I hadn't been experiencing much in the way of symptoms, beyond a general feeling of sluggishness. Still, I went in for a typical well-woman exam at the medical center.

For a long time before then, I'd been overweight. Throughout much of my youth, I'd ignored my weight and coasted along on my God-given energy. But as I got out of college, my weight caught up to me. I was struggling with it day to day, sometimes moment to moment. I liked food. I also liked being effective at work and in my personal life, and I had to admit I was beginning to feel bogged down, like my real self had been replaced with a giant anchor. So I booked the exam.

The doctor examined me, then looked up and made eye contact. "We have a problem here," she said. She told me I had stage one cervical cancer, which was very treatable. But given the loop it threw me for, I could only imagine what it felt like to receive a graver diagnosis. My self-esteem plummeted straight into the toilet. Generally, except for smokers, I didn't see cancer as a disease someone could blame themselves for getting.

One of the many things my father always told me was to never, ever get into the energy business. Of course, that's exactly what I did.

I was alone in a new city, with a new job where I wanted to do well and a long-term relationship receding in my rear-view mirror. At that time, you could comfortably label me a hot mess. Because of that, I decided to go through the whole thing alone. I didn't call my parents. I didn't tell a friend. I embraced the strange newness of my Houston environment, complete with its state-of-the-art medical service, tucked my head down, and dealt with it. I didn't have any true local friends, just work acquaintances. Oddly, although going it alone isn't something I recommend, my approach to my illness suited my needs at the time. After all, I got to keep my rosy narrative intact in the eyes of the outside world. New beginning, new job, new city—I'd sailed off into the sunset, right? Nuh-uh.

My treatment lasted twelve weeks and was designed to aggressively knock the thing clean out of my system. Of course, my insurance company decided I should foot the bill alone, so in addition to my medical battle, I waged a legal one against my insurance company.

It was like the whole Houston thing was doomed to fail. Adding insult to injury, just one year after I'd started at Enron, I was laid off there too. Relationship, job, clean bill of health—all taken away from me at rapid speed. Welcome to Houston, Katie.

In retrospect, my choice to battle the illness alone wasn't merely about me wanting to look strong. It also was tied up in shame. Such was my mindset at the time.

In the course of dealing with it on my own (though I did eventually tell my parents), I learned a great deal about myself. Except I didn't learn your standard cancer patient lessons about strength and fortitude. Sure, I learned I could handle it. But I also learned that I was a less-than-open person. I put image before reality. I was out to impress rather than express. I was determined not only to battle cancer, but to edit it out of my life narrative.

Which is why, when the cancer later returned, it made sense. The cancer had more to teach me. And the second time around, I was more receptive to it.

Cervical cancer revisited me in 2014. That year, Pink Petro was coming into focus, and I was operating with a clearer and stronger sense of purpose. In the meantime, I had a husband and child, so I wasn't about to hide my disease from anyone.

This wasn't just a matter of being open about it within my household; it was a matter of knowing that what I'd thought had worked before hadn't worked at all. Grinning and bearing it is no wise substitute for hugging somebody and crying it out. For me, the key distinction between those two reactions was the ability to stop blaming myself for my cancer.

Meanwhile, I had a fire in my belly to go out into the world and do something different. I was more aligned to my personal sense of meaning. Meaning certainly keeps you warm at night—and keeps you strong when facing your mortality. In fact, mortality is meaning's bitch. Meaning looks at mortality and says, "You may come and claim me someday—and that may even be sometime soon—but at least when you come, I'll have been up to something awesome. And although you can take me, you can't take that away from me."

I felt lucky in a way. Unlike many others who've dealt with cancer, I'd had the benefit of a live dress rehearsal. It wasn't, "Oh, no—the damn thing's back!" It was, "No worries, I've been down this road before." I knew how to navigate it now that I knew my meaning, and thereby knew myself. The first time around, I hadn't known either. The second time around? There I was. And the lucky part about my round two is that it wasn't as serious. After a procedure, I've been free for nearly five years. Cancer taught me to embrace life.

Growing up, through a million tiny signals and messages, I was trained to care about what other people think. For a long time, it was my number-one flaw. It's not at the top of my list anymore, but it's still on there. I care, at times way too much.

But as I've accumulated life experiences, I've accepted that I'm human, just like everyone else, complete with upsides and downsides. If I'm not somebody's cup of tea, it's their loss, because I am who I am. Trying to be who you're not aligns you to all the wrong people. You're selling people a lie, and you probably won't like the people who show up at your door. They're showing up for something fake— something you're struggling to keep intact, for fear they'll reject the real you.

> **As I've accumulated life experiences, I've accepted that I'm human, just like everyone else, complete with upsides and downsides. If I'm not somebody's cup of tea, it's their loss, because I am who I am.**

In time, I became better at showing my real self to other people. Not only was the truth of who I am easier to remember, but it was a better platform for all the things I have to offer. If you create something while you're living a lie, it's not the real you who's creating. It's a character, a version of yourself, who keeps your creation too many degrees away from the truth of who you are. Instead, just create what you want. If it's truthful, other people will not only resonate with it, but they'll fall on their knees with gratitude because your truth empowers other people's truth.

People get lonely easily. So much is expected of us, whether that's acting a certain way, rising to a certain level, or meeting or exceeding people's expectations. This efficiently cuts us off from the truth of who we are. But if we block out all that noise—all the expectations—and simply express our own authentic hearts, our place in the world will become clear in the snap of a finger. It is as if we're Bruce Willis in *The Sixth Sense*, not realizing until now that we've been dead.

But we're not dead. We're still here. We're only wasting time by being anything less than wholly, incredibly truthful.

Chapter Four

A TALE OF TWO LAYOFFS

"If it comes down to your ethics
versus a job, choose ethics. You
can always find another job."

—SALLIE KRAWCHECK

Remember when I told you about my pair of layoffs? Much like my pair of cancer experiences, my two layoffs found me in pretty different frames of mind. Which is a good thing because the difference indicates growth.

Now, how does a person actually get laid off? What does it look like in the room when it's happening? In the first case, in 1998, someone handed me a box. "Pack your stuff" was the message.

The "good" news was that the company let go of about a hundred people that day. Clearly, something was going on there, and generally in a layoff, that's all it is: money. That didn't stop me from making it all about me. I remember crying my whole way out the door. I had only been there a year, but I was one of the hardest workers there. I piled on so much extra time. I always found myself looking around at the slackers, wondering how *they* managed to hang on, and now I was among those being cut. Newsflash, young Katie: life's not fair! This was a pivotal moment, as not only was it my very first layoff experience, but it was my first and only real job outside of college so far.

> **Early on in my business life, I was lucky to learn the value of being community oriented. It's good to be connected. Simply knowing people, interacting with them, and keeping up with what they're doing grants countless advantages in terms of opportunity.**

Months later, the company was investigated for fraud. Thereafter, it went into bankruptcy and sold off its assets. Ironically, when I was laid off, my superiors involved security, escorting everyone out as if we were the ones who'd done something wrong. Obviously, the company was up to no good, but rather than own up to it and clean up shop, it did the cheap thing and made its workers feel like criminals.

What made no sense at the time makes perfect sense now: the problem was with the company, not with me.

Early on in my business life, I was lucky to learn the value of being community oriented. It's good to be connected. Simply knowing people, interacting with them, and keeping up with what they're doing grants countless advantages in terms of opportunity. At the time of my layoff, I had a network; I had been lucky to be elected to the board of directors of the Direct Marketing Association of St. Louis. Even though we weren't yet in the twenty-first century, I was a digitally minded person and ahead of the curve in terms of computers and other technology. I had the privilege of being the youngest person elected to this board, which was fun and empowering on one hand, but perhaps rocking the boat on the other.

My friend and mentor Lori Feldman was an in-strumental player in my life at the time. She always felt like a big sister to me. She saw a lot in me that I, as a younger person, simply couldn't see in myself, and she always pushed me forward. I looked up to her as a profoundly powerful and successful busi-nesswoman, and I never imagined I could be like her someday. Lori didn't see it that way; she advocated for me when others couldn't see my potential. She was a sponsor for me.

Courtesy of my board position and Lori's fervent support, I landed a great marketing technology role with a DMA member company and division of General Motors called GMAC Insurance. My network had paid off and I was back on my feet. Once again, I was the youngster coming in to make changes. This company was just getting into e-commerce, email, and digital marketing, and I helped it through the transition. Insurance, like energy, isn't a sexy subject, but I was determined to leverage technology to bring GMAC Insurance to the next level. Vice President Janet Bourne, a woman I admired and one of the only female leaders at her level in the company, gave me great support. Janet played the game well, and she always appreciated her people—she was one of the few leaders I worked for in my early career whom I really appreciated. She always embraced new ideas, and her door was always open.

In the meantime, I started keeping an eye on a guy named Seth Godin. By now, you've probably heard of him as the father of permission and purpose-driven marketing. Back in 1998, he was just some guy named Seth, but he talked about things that hit me—namely that in direct marketing, personalization is key. In other words, don't market to the whole world; it's too broad. Zero in on your audience. Be personal. Be niche. Seth was all over this mindset.

Then Y2K cropped up. Everyone was worried about what life would be like when the clock struck midnight on January 1, 2000. People had been predicting anarchy, but when the turn of the century happened, it was uneventful.

When it was finally my time to leave GMAC, it was of my own accord. Other exciting stuff around St. Louis grabbed my attention, such as a well-funded start-up that was getting its beak wet in the vast sea of the internet. Never mind that Jeff Bezos was launching Amazon's IPO; I was getting my own piece of the digital action at a company called Primary Webworks. I was kind of a girl Friday: project manager, marketing person, even salesperson. We landed many great consumer clients—I worked with Ralston Purina, Mastercard, and even had a taste of beer (I mean work) at Anheuser Busch. I was the hands and heart and mind of the company. I wasn't running the joint, sure, but I was up to many cool things.

That was when I got the call to move to Houston.

I'd never given the energy business much thought. I'd had my eye on the likes of Amazon and Yahoo! The early internet was a fascinating place. Coming from my Louisiana upbringing, Silicon Valley seemed like some strange new planet dropped right onto America. Cool things were happening. I sensed even then that the internet could disrupt commerce. For one thing, delivery timeframes would shorten, and life in general—in the world, in the mind—was bound to go much faster. Everything seemed to be speeding up.

But as we've discussed, the company courting me was Enron (more specifically, it was an entity institutionally owned by Enron). The company offered to double my current pay. Every cell in my body knew I'd be a fool to say no. But in the back of my mind, I heard my dad talking. He'd lost his engineering job in the oil and gas business in the 1980s. His unemployment wasn't a fleeting window of time; it was a meaningful interlude in my childhood. When he wasn't working, my mom was. It fell on her to hold down the household. In the '80s, that was rare. And while my dad's unemployment wasn't forever, my mother being the breadwinner during his layoff definitely shaped my rearing.

I remembered my dad talking about how unpredictable the energy business was. But then again, so was I! Every time my dad gave me a message, he somehow simultaneously sent a counter-message.

It's not that I didn't take his warning seriously, but I also remembered something else he said throughout my childhood, something perhaps less weighty but equally meaningful: "Turn the lights off, Katie! Don't waste energy!"

Whoa, I'd think, *energy runs the world.*

When Enron came knocking, I wanted in. I was fascinated with how technology could interact with business and commerce, and the energy business seemed to be such a hotbed of activity that the mere idea of being in it lit up my entire grid.

Anyway, we all know what happened at Enron. I was actually at the meeting when Jeffrey Skilling, the now-infamous CEO, stepped down. His official word was that he was taking time off to be with his family. In his place, CEO Kenneth Lay stepped up to the plate, which, unbeknownst to me at the time, would be a harbinger of doom.

First, unrelated to Enron but in keeping with 2001's overall grim nature, 9/11 happened. I was in Downtown Houston, on the trade floor, when the Twin Towers were hit. All of us became nervous because we too worked in a dual-tower structure, so our bosses promptly sent us home and told us to stock up on gas and cash. We were convinced the world was ending.

But not quite. The end of *our* world came a few weeks later, in October and November. We were told we wouldn't be working soon; a mass layoff was in progress. Still, for the time being, we went to work. Oddly, even though our company was owned by Enron, we got more news on the outside than we ever did on the inside. Employees had to watch the news to catch up on what was happening right under their noses. When it finally happened, Enron's collapse was a major milestone. It was something of a #MeToo revelation for its time: an unveiling of corruption that we all knew was widespread, but never expected to be called out and punished, much less look so ugly in the light of day.

When the layoffs happened, I remember looking at the traders, who'd been paused as if by remote control. One moment, they were trading; the next, they weren't allowed to because the market froze Enron's credit. It was a bizarre scenario, this hollow, halting moment. A bunch of the traders (all men) went across the street for pizza, and I went along. They decided to bring the pizza back, roll a keg out onto the floor, and start drinking. None of our leaders were explaining what was happening. We were like a bunch of kids waiting for our parents to pick us up.

Little by little, we got word that we should come into the building to collect our personal items. I wondered what would be next; because I was classified as a consultant, I wasn't sure how the layoff pertained to me on a technical level. I just knew this was the craziest thing I'd ever seen.

Our competitors had some good laughs at our expense, and the press was interested in what we had to say. Workers' names showed up on media call lists. I remember getting contacted by the *National Enquirer* to get the scoop and thinking, *Here I am again, unemployed.* But like I said before, there was a difference this time: I knew what had happened had nothing to do with me.

You might think the opposite was likely, that I'd wonder why I kept getting laid off. Thankfully, my consciousness pivoted in the other direction, and I simply realized neither layoff was my fault. That's not to say I wasn't responsible for my own path, but there's a fine line between responsibility and blame. While I knew I could learn something valuable from this, my lesson was not that I was somehow irreparably flawed. So I asked myself what I could do to avoid being laid off again, and the answer came clear as day: work for companies that align with my values. In other words: *culture is everything.*

It's easier said than done, of course, to work for companies that align with your values. Back then, we didn't have the internet or social media to help gauge our employers' reputations. It took me time to get the whole values thing under control. First, there were my layoffs. Soon, I would be treated to my very own Donald Trump moment; I would be told, "You're fired."

> **In my twenties, I figured if I was smart, effective, useful, and a go-getter, everyone would love me. Except I'm a frickin' hurricane. Hurricane Harvey may have been rough, but Hurricane Katie is a whole other story. I'm like, "You want change? I'm your girl!" I went in there unleashing mad fury, kicking ass, taking names—and getting knocked flat on my face.**

I was in my mid-twenties when I got a job offer from a private sporting goods company, your standard mom-and-pop operation. Unlike a publicly traded company, it wasn't subject to strict regulations, so things were more casual there. I went for the job, and I took a pay cut. I was hired to work in IT and help transform the business. I figured I might return to the energy sector someday, but for now, why not have a little side adventure in retail? I thought, *Who knows? I might even get a hunting license!*

It didn't take long for me to realize the whole thing was a joke. For starters, some of the folks in leadership were complete dinosaurs. While their mouths spoke of change, their actions spoke of inertia. Their main objective was to maintain the status quo at all costs—which is not to say these people were evil, at least not fully. They *thought* they wanted to change, but when they saw what actual change entailed, things got dicey.

For me, this job was a wake-up call about the nature of office politics. In my twenties, I figured if I was smart, effective, useful, and a go-getter, everyone would love me. Except I'm a frickin' hurricane. Hurricane Harvey may have been rough, but Hurricane Katie is a whole other story. I'm like, "You want change? I'm your girl!" I went in there unleashing mad fury, kicking ass, taking names—and getting knocked flat on my face.

My first overt adversary came in the form of a crusty old guy. For storytelling purposes, I will nickname him Crusty Guy. One day, Crusty Guy emailed me a penis joke. This was before the age of texting, when the mere act of emailing gave people an adrenaline rush. But I didn't find his email funny. *He* thought it was funny, as did others around the office, but I wasn't about to accept it as normal.

So I brought it to my supervisor's attention. We'll call her Jellyfish. This was a woman of vast morality. The only problem was, what she had in sheer values, she lacked in terms of a human spine. She wouldn't take the matter upstairs; she wanted to keep the peace. I was my own lone advocate in the office.

The next thing I knew, I was called into the CIO's office. Jellyfish was there beside him. The two of them handed me a crisp official letter. This wasn't yet my Donald Trump moment, but it was the seed that grew the flower. According to the letter, I was creating an unproductive work environment. My chief crime, which went unstated, was that I had failed to laugh at Crusty Guy's supposedly well-intentioned penis joke. The letter stated that I had ninety days to turn my act around. So I threw a smile on my face. On the outside, I was all good cheer, ready to rock 'n' roll.

Behind the scenes, I cried about it. Never had I been so unfairly disciplined in the workplace. Sure, I'd had my share of reviews, complete with a bit of backhanded feedback ("Yes, you're a go-getter—but we really need you to take it down a notch!"). But this? This was an all-out ambush.

Meanwhile, it occurred to me that Crusty Guy had other reasons to resent me. He'd wanted to be in charge of choosing whoever was ultimately hired for my role (me), but that honor had gone to a female colleague. Whoops, poor male ego.

In any case, I was now hard at work on my personal performance improvement plan (my PIP). Essentially, I was on probation. Still, I believed logic, reason, and a dutiful adherence to the facts would eventually pay off in my favor. So at the start of those ninety days, I got to work doing what my past experience had trained me to do: gather feedback.

I created my own SurveyMonkey, and I went around the whole department, conducting a 360. Nowadays, that's common, but it wasn't at the time. I asked senior people, my peers, and my subordinates what they thought of how I was doing, inviting them to offer criticism and emphasizing my openness to dialogue. I then marched my results into my boss's office. My reviews were glowing—I was untouchable, unassailable, armed with airtight arguments and five-star Yelp reviews before Yelp had even been invented. Not only that, but I'd gone extracurricular and hired a coach. I was intent on mastering this terrain, to the point where it'd be hard to tell the difference between me and a sterling-silver shooting star.

It didn't take long to receive my first demotion after that. I was first reassigned to special projects, which is code for "nothing special." On one project, I was replaced by one of Crusty Guy's subordinates. Being disciplined had been sudden and jarring; being benched was more gradual and insidious.

Meanwhile, my gallbladder—evidently studying

to be a master of good timing—took it upon itself to burst, leading to an emergency surgery. So there I was, working hard to recover my health while preserving my job. Fortunately, I achieved the former, but not the latter. One day, as I approached my desk, my boss was already waiting for me there. Next to her was the head of security. "We're gonna go to the CIO's office," she said.

Upon our arrival—BOOM! Pure Donald Trump: "You're fired." I was told I hadn't done well and had only created more conflict in our workplace. I was overcome with jitters, but I kept them hidden. I thanked them, smiled, and shook their hands. "Thank you for this experience," I said. I grabbed the box of my packed-up things they had ready for me (flashback to my first layoff), and security escorted me to my car. There, when I was finally alone, I came to pieces.

Crying like a baby, I called my dad. My dad, as you might have gathered, is a classic Southern guy: straightforward, but not without a strong touch of poetry. I'll never forget what he told me: "Katie, you've been laid off, you've been fired . . . Now you can put 'Seasoned' on your resume."

There it was: the perspective I needed in the lowest, crappiest depths of a dire day. Because without that experience and what it taught me, I wouldn't have been nearly as focused on my values in the days that followed.

In many cases, working for companies that align with your values simply means becoming an entrepreneur. After all, when you work for yourself, the values and the company tend to be a single, cohesive entity.

But whether you're an employee or an entrepreneur, the lesson holds just as much water. Plenty of companies will align with your values, and it makes no difference what those values are, new or old, high or low, weird or conventional. It's like with dating: Somebody out there is bound to like and accept you, and vice versa.

When you're young and experimenting, the search is murky. You don't yet know exactly who you are, much less what you stand for and how much you are willing to take until you break. You might be clear on some values, but your core values will take time to materialize. As such, the only way to discover them is through a game of matching and mismatching. You'll know it when you feel it. Sometimes it clicks; other times it's off. Like I've noted, back then we didn't have Google, LinkedIn, or Glassdoor. You had to possess a sixth sense and just go for it.

In a disempowered mindset, your superiors set the

tone in terms of values at work, and you have to do your best to put up with whatever they dish out. But values are personal and come from within; you alone must identify what's important to you. In my case, it was the basics: honesty, integrity, coherency, a clear mission, and a sense of meaning and real connection.

Enron wasn't a home to such things; it was a place where corruption had taken hold. Enron took short-cuts and fooled the market so well with its shadiness that it graced the covers of every major magazine. And it was a tragedy—I saw lives get destroyed; people lost fortunes; marriages went under; former leaders I'd admired ended their own lives. Kenneth Lay died before his conviction, but he likely wouldn't have been living comfortably if he had lived. Since the scandal broke nearly twenty years ago, Jeffrey Skilling was let out of jail on good behavior in 2019. Andrew Fastow, the former CFO who cooked the books, was released in 2011. Both men regularly speak about the lessons they learned.

Being nonjudgmental is not my way of condoning corruption; it's simply my way of emphasizing that you alone know where you belong. You'll probably feel it in the pit of your stomach. You'll get a feel for your workplace and its people and processes first— and thereafter, in due course, you'll get a feel for the underlying and overlying values.

So how's your stomach feeling now? If the values

aren't telling with who you are, this is a marriage that is meant to fail. Values are never light or flexible; they go to the core of who you are. Sometimes, yes, you can gain from contrast. Sometimes you'll need a partner who's a little more square or round so that between you a balance is struck.

But on a company-wide level, if your values mismatch, eventually one of you will have to go. In my case, three times, the companies proved rotten from the inside and my end points there were but the snapping of a branch before the whole tree toppled. How could I have avoided such a fate? By simply avoiding the rot. Live and learn. Go and grow. Grow with the flow.

From my firing onward, whenever I looked for work, right up until I started my own company, I looked for values at the forefront. They matter more than the very mechanics of the job itself. For example, if you're a natural-born shoemaker working at a shop that's misaligned with your core values, then you're way better off being a bootmaker for a shop with which you align.

Yeah, you'll be surprised. It'll be like, "Wow! Boots? I never knew that was my calling." But the job itself is secondary; the values come first, each and every time. With the right ones in place, you can actually grow forward and thrive.

Chapter Five

BE A WEIRDO

"Why fit in when you were
born to stand out?"

—DR. SEUSS

Speaking of your values, they play a big role in helping you find your tribe. It took me a long time to
find mine. I was an oddball growing up—I had big
and unconventional ideas that people didn't always
understand. When I shared them at school, in equal
measure, I stood out as a teacher's pet as much as a
target for my peers to pick on. In those years, I was
constantly weighing my intellect against my desire
to fit in.

I've long believed that the more open you are to
getting feedback from other people, the stronger you
become as a person. If you take in feedback, you get
to know yourself and what the world makes of you.
You learn where you rise, where you fall, and where
you can stand to make improvements. You also

become self-aware enough to know that you are, of course, a weirdo.

As all weirdos can attest, we tend to be misunderstood. When you're a weirdo—when there's only one person like you—people can't readily shove you into a box to make your personality and motives coherent. Adding to my weirdo-ness in my early career was the fact that I was outspoken and I knew what I wanted. This didn't mean I wanted to step on people's toes, but when I did, it was because I was just being myself and other people didn't know what to make of me. As I grew up, I realized this was an aspect of myself I had to get under control. It wasn't about conforming or caring what other people thought of me. It was more about being able to navigate the world with full awareness of how I came off and what my strengths were.

Early in my career, I was an alienated soul. I'd grown accustomed to being a weirdo, so I'd censor my own ideas because they'd earned me a lot of bad feedback in the past. But self-censoring doesn't feel good for very long. Nobody thrives in their own suppression. Our ideas, good or bad, are designed to be expressed. So what was the solution? It all came down to being around people who appreciated that I was different.

That seems obvious in theory, but it's difficult to pull off in day-to-day life. As I matured, I began looking at the world through a 95/5 paradigm. It seemed clear that 95 percent of the world doesn't care about doing anything other than falling in line and following the status quo. Then there's the other 5 percent, who want to break out of the tested parameters. These are the seekers, the weirdos, the visionaries— the ones who actually push things forward and leave change on this planet after they're gone. They care.

> **I've long believed that the more open you are to getting feedback from other people, the stronger you become as a person. If you take in feedback, you get to know yourself and what the world makes of you. You learn where you rise, where you fall, and where you can stand to make improvements. You also become self-aware enough to know that you are, of course, a weirdo.**

The 5 percent is an exclusive club, not only one everybody yearns to be a part of, but one many people pretend to belong to even when they don't. It's not my place to judge who's in or out, but a ton of people talk a good game in terms of how original they are while shying away from originality every chance they get.

As those in the true 5 percent know, it can be a lonely place. You're stuck with yourself and the great, big freak that you are. It's lonely not only in terms of lacking friends and allies, but also in terms of attracting enemies. For years, growing up, I was bullied by people who wanted me to stop thinking differently. "Katie," they said, "why can't you just be in this neat old box?" Believe me, I tried. I shoved myself into the proverbial box, reluctant to think even an inch outside it. But it was overwhelmingly painful. This experience accumulated into a wall, one I subconsciously built around myself. I'd absorbed the lesson that being outspoken was taboo—something that worked better in private than in public. Much of the time, it wasn't even advisable in private. The message I received about it was loud and clear—and also very tied up in the fact that I was a girl: "That's not for you to worry about."

That's precisely how mediocrity perpetuates. Because human social interactions repeat this pattern constantly in trillions of little ways, people—particularly women—are left with a choice: either go along to get along . . . or rise up and make your voice heard.

The latter sounds oh-so-sexy and amazing, but it's actually terrifying. When you're a woman, you're either outward or inward. Sure, countless women are somewhere in between, but the general push against your voice is so hard and endless that when you push back, it draws attention.

> **Adding to my weirdo-ness in my early career was the fact that I was outspoken and I knew what I wanted. This didn't mean I wanted to step on people's toes, but when I did, it was because I was just being myself and other people didn't know what to make of me.**

In the end, as I've said, it all comes down to searching the planet for those with whom you resonate. When I discovered Sheryl Sandberg's work and the *Lean In* community, for example, I reached a whole new level of personal liberation. Needless to say, I've put Sheryl on a pedestal, and when you do that, you never think you'll meet that person in real life. But little by little, I started moving in that direction.

First, I followed her on Facebook. Then, thinking, *Hey, I'm gonna start this business,* I joined a Lean In Circle. I figured I'd benefit from being around like-minded people, ones off of whom I could bounce my ideas. Upon joining the circle, I found myself becoming more and more a fan of the group each time I inter-acted with it. I needed it; it became a fixture of my working and personal lives. Sheryl was all about com-munication and connection: showing up, being heard, getting your message across. Looking back, I see how my involvement in the Lean In Circle was interwoven with my launch of Pink Petro and Experience Energy.

Sheryl's second book, *Option B*, published in 2017 after her husband's death, was about loss, resilience, and being tough. In it, Sheryl wrote that it's okay to grieve, cry, and let out your emotions, but you also have to make the most of whatever it is you have to work with. That year, during Sheryl's tour for the book, which hooked up with various Lean In Circles across the country, I had the chance to meet her on two occasions. The first one, in April, was almost two years to the day following her husband's death and, as it would turn out, a few months before Hurricane Harvey. Our encounter was brief. I'd have to wait un-til August to *really* meet her, just weeks prior to the storm that changed my life forever.

In reaction to both her books, Sheryl faced criti-cism of her privilege. With *Lean In*, people said she didn't share the same barriers as women of color and other minorities. With *Option B*, she was told that al-though she might have weathered loss, she still had millions of dollars with which to insulate herself. To me, this was all lazy dehumanization. It was almost as though, by revealing so much of her humanity, Sheryl faced the bewildering phenomenon of other people scrambling to take it away.

I wasn't in that crowd. I felt close to her message, and to her. She had taught me to find my voice. She had told me, "It's okay. You're not crazy. You have big things to do." Nowadays, I ask every woman I meet what she would do if she were not afraid.

The second time I met Sheryl, there was more of a buildup. My daughter, Ally, was in on the whole thing, running around and saying, "Mommy's gonna meet Ms. Sheryl! Mommy's gonna meet Ms. Sheryl!" Oh, I'd told her all about Ms. Sheryl, and now I would be heading to Ms. Sheryl's home for a Lean In leader celebration.

Naturally, when you visit someone's home, the appropriate etiquette is to bring a gift. But the question is, what do you bring to the woman who has everything? Well, Ally's really into superheroes—she's a total Ninja Turtle–type kid—and she had a clear sense of what Sheryl was all about. In her mind, she'd already framed her as a superhero. "Every superhero needs a fidget spinner," she said.

Hmm, she had a point. I could give Sheryl the fidget spinner while crediting my adorable kid with the idea, and I wouldn't be straining to make some big monetary statement. My gift would have actual substance, along with a giant compliment. Still, in order to follow through on this, I had to step into my big-girl pants. The idea, being so high concept, could backfire. Yet because it was original, it kept floating to the top of my list of options.

When the day finally came, I entered Sheryl's home holding Ally's fidget spinner. All the other women in attendance had gifts too—Tiffany boxes and other fancy and delectable choices.

"Is this your first time coming here?" I asked the other women around me, nervously holding my gift. A lot of them said yes. I started building a mental wall and asked them if I should follow through on my gift idea. Uniformly, they were not only all for it, but they thought it was amazing. Phew.

At this point, I had none other than Sheryl's words to guide me: What would you do if you weren't afraid? So, I went for it. When I handed her the fidget spinner, Sheryl asked how old Ally was. Smiling, I said, "Six." We chatted about our prior encounter in Houston, and she could not have been more warm or receptive. I was smitten. Hero vibes crawled all over me. Like any true hero, she showed gratitude, but I was most grateful to Ally for the master plan.

A month went by, and my Lean In community was getting bigger. Word got around that the Lean In

Foundation was looking to grant ten large circles the ability to start their own nonprofit. Right away, that lit up my grid. I thought it would be a tremendous way to give back. So I got the nonprofit application, took it home, and told myself I'd sit down later and look at it. But that never happened. Hurricane Harvey happened instead.

I was in the darkest of dark moments in my life. I felt like I'd been robbed of my breath. I was out looking for a home, trying to resuscitate my business, and working harder than ever before. That's something I've noticed about myself: when the big storms come, I dig in and work harder. This isn't about strength for me; it's about keeping my head down and pushing forward. It's my way of reacting, coping, and growing with the flow. I'll cry, sure, and I will stagnate at times. But my work will be there as a form of lubrication, greasing the tracks and allowing me forward momentum.

As such, my whole world after Harvey boiled down to Facebook communications, community rallying, and supply facilitation. Amid the storm of work that followed the storm from the sky, one day I got a very sweet and simple note from people at the Lean In Foundation. They wanted to let me know the work I was doing was important and necessary. They reminded me I needed to keep going and growing.

Man, did this weirdo need to hear that at the time. Through Lean In, I viscerally learned that we must all help and support each other. It's simple to say but hard to actually understand. Just like the old expression "All ships rise with the tide," when the storms of life come, that tide gets challenging. And it's then, most of all, when you need friends around you, which makes it all the better for your ship to rise.

We're in life alone: our oddness, our uniqueness, our perspectives, our singular points of view. The more novel and outside the box we are, the more society will try to shake us off like a case of fleas. What would you do if you weren't afraid? Ask yourself that question every day and then go and do what makes you most afraid. The world needs your strength, your ideas, and more weirdos. "Why fit in when you are born to stand out?" asks Dr. Seuss.

That's where validation comes in. Validation is the traction that allows outsiders like us to hang on. Validation also grants us the permission to unleash our inner strength and grow.

If we're lost, we're not just on the wrong ground; we're probably not receiving proper validation. Somebody needs to see us with clarity and advise us on where we can best go to thrive in full.

Get away from the ones who don't validate you. Stick with those who do.

Chapter Six

SHARKS IN
THE WATER

"If people throw stones at you, pick
'em up and build something."

—LECRAE

Being a weirdo means you meet your fair share of
bullies. Back when I was a kid, bullies had to work
a lot harder than they do now. Bullying was sort of
a contact sport, taking place face-to-face instead
of on the internet. Sure, you could prank call people or sign them up for a thousand phony magazine
subscriptions, but in general, if you wanted to bully
someone, you had to roll up your sleeves and do it in
person, typically on the schoolyard.

Nowadays, bullying is much easier to do online,
and thus much more prevalent. It must have been
a good day for bullies when they realized they no
longer had to extend themselves as much. It was the
same day, of course, the internet was invented.

Back in 1987, when I was twelve, there was no such thing as Facebook, Twitter, cell phones, or what have you. You know what we had instead? Garbage cans.

Yep, the girl in my school who bullied people threw them in the garbage can. I call this old-school trolling; it was way more personal than the cyberbullying we've grown accustomed to. When someone stuffs you in a garbage can, it has a certain stench of intimacy—and not just the intimacy of physical contact, as disturbing as that is. Old-school trolling was intimate in that it was targeted. Online bullies can cast wide nets and quickly harass two dozen people between when they wake up and when they make it downstairs for their morning cereal. Old-school bullies, anchored in the physical world, had less time, less bandwidth, and thus fewer options available. They had to be mindful about picking their victims. In order to inflict maximum pain and damage, they had to make sure they were picking out somebody they could have a good, awful time with.

In keeping with my garbage bully's style, she had earned me a memorable nickname in middle school: Garbage Girl. According to my classmates, I smelled like garbage—and I looked like it too. No amount of soap or hair gel could rectify the situation. Once the name was on me, it stuck, not unlike garbage itself. Day in and day out, I knew my destination was not just school, but the garbage can. Garbage Girl. Garbage can.

I had many bullies back then—if you were cool, I was your ideological opponent—but my main bully's name was Sherry. I knew her terrain of attack was the girl's room, so I tried to change up my routines. I always went to different bathrooms, which granted me a 50-percent shot of avoiding her. But for the most part, Sherry had her way, and into the garbage can I went.

Finally, I told my dad about it. Talk about old school: he told me to fight back. He said that when somebody treats you like that, you're well within your right to haul off and knock back. Anti-bullying tactics were a little more straightforward back then.

Dad's words didn't sink in easily. After all, he and my mom had always taught me to be a kind, loving pacifist, but now he was sending me a counter-message. Hitting back sounded horrific, even if that person was causing me distress. But the more I thought about my dad's instructions, the more empowered I became, not because I wanted to hit somebody, but because I knew he had my back. Psychologically, that makes an enormous difference to somebody being bullied. A key facet of victimization is isolation; bullies target loners and weirdos—people without a posse. But my dad was conveying that he was my posse, and it felt good to know someone would be in my corner if push came to literal shove.

One day soon after that, I got on the bus. Classically, the cool kids sat in the back, and I sat in the front to evade their harassment. At school that day, I eventually had to use the bathroom to change during gym class. Everything in me wanted to avoid a confrontation, so this time I went into the boys' room. It was a radical departure, one that could possibly lead to other kinds of trouble, but I didn't care. I just didn't want the garbage can.

Bullies are predators; when it comes to tracking their prey, they're known to go out of their way if they have to. Of course, Sherry and her crew caught on, and they showed up in the boys' room. My dad's instructions echoed in my head. This time, when they came at me, I swung back. I took them by complete surprise.

That's another thing about bullies: they're easily surprised. They're often so certain of their superiority that when one of their victims stands up to them, it shatters their whole worldview. That's what happened to Sherry that day. I not only swung back, but I did so in front of the boys. Oh, it was a good show—and a just one, at that. The boys laughed about it for days. For a short while, I was a hero. I learned that in order to beat bullies, you have to beat them at their own game.

Nowadays, we're told the opposite, to avoid bullies, which is easier to do online. Bullies will be wherever you go online, but you can block and report them one at a time. That's a reasonable solution, but not always a sustainable one. Blocking a bully doesn't repair your reputation as prey, which in the eyes of some will remain fully intact, thus possibly perpetuating the victimization cycle. Meanwhile, avoidance is just not a tenable tool for living. Those who avoid bad things have a way of growing weaker, not stronger, as time goes by.

Beating bullies at their own game doesn't require violence, but as mentioned, it does require a posse. If your kid is being bullied, they might simply require more and/or better friends. If you are the one being bullied, maybe your network needs to be beefed up. Take a look at your corner. Who's in it? How strong are they? That corner needs to be stocked with resilience and muscle.

Once you've established a posse, putting you on more level ground with potential bullies while reducing your vulnerability, then it's all about beating them at whatever game they're playing. If you're dealing with an online troll who gets their kicks from your defensive and/or emotional reaction, then the wisdom "Don't feed the trolls" absolutely applies: Deprive them of what they want. Ignore them. They are not worth it. But if your bully uses other forms of engagement—involving fists or money or sexuality or power games—you're more likely to have to go toe to toe.

I know these words might sound controversial, and I know disengaging—or peacefully protesting—is more fashionable these days, but let's try a mental exercise. Let's look at how Donald Trump got into office in 2016. He started by rewriting the rule book. He gave his opponents demeaning nicknames. He issued provocative, insulting, and outright hateful proclamations one after the other. He acted crazy. He became a master of saying what one wasn't supposed to say. Nobody expected him to win—except, of course, the sixty-two million Americans who voted for him. He pulled it off by stooping lower than anyone imagined possible, playing a crude, harsh game all by himself. His opponents could not keep up; they tried to aim high and keep it classy, not realizing how much momentum he was gaining down there in the dirt.

Now, imagine if some bold soul had suddenly started hitting back on Trump's level: cruel nicknames, rude jokes, outrageous comebacks, insane, headline-grabbing statements. Trump would have been left with his head spinning. He not only would have been surprised and hard-pressed to keep up, but he would have resented his methods being stolen right in plain sight. That resentment would have led to anger, which would have scrambled up his whole game. He wouldn't be the lone dark horse out there spouting addictive nonsense and keeping the media glued to him. No, he would have had an actual opponent to deal with.

Hindsight is always twenty-twenty. It's easy to call out mistakes when looking in the rearview mirror. The president's communication tactics were so absurd to most of us that there didn't seem to be any need to beat him at his own game. Now there is, though, isn't there?

It's a drag to have to stoop down to a bully's level. It shouldn't be necessary. It casts light on the worst parts of ourselves: the base impulses, the rage, the raw animal stuff that we try to tell ourselves we've outgrown. But, on the other hand, when we beat bullies at their own game, we gain a lot in the process: self-respect, for starters, and a sense of our own strength too. And, most valuable of all, the knowledge that—when push comes to shove—we are actually able to win the fight.

It didn't happen overnight, but I've reached a point in my personal evolution where I think you simply have to confront things and call them out. Leaving them buried is contrary to truth. Naturally, you still have to pick your battles, and there's no need to turn every tiff into an altercation. But if somebody's objective is to throw you in the garbage can, you have every right to stop that nonsense.

Over time, as both target and witness, I've become an expert on how bullies' minds work, which is useful for combating them. Because, don't forget, the bully isn't showing you who they really are. No, the bully's out to paint a distorted picture that front-loads their strength to draw attention away from their weaknesses. Do this enough days in a row, in front of enough people who seem weaker than you, and perhaps the illusion of strength may start bearing resemblance to the real thing. Regardless, an illusion is exactly what it remains.

It's not that bullies are weak, per se. Like all human beings, they have their strengths and weaknesses. What distinguishes them more is actually a weak sense of their own identity. Trolls are like this too—and you better believe trolling is but another form of bullying. It goes like this: A bully (or troll) isn't sure who they really are. As such, they aren't sure what they're good at. The value picture is hazy for them, maybe because of how they were raised, maybe because of plain old low self-esteem. But when it comes to identity, these folks aren't running particularly hot.

Then the bully steps out into the world and

encounters other people who actually know who they are. By no measure are these people perfect, but they're solid enough in the identity department to feel like a threat to the bully. And the bully, overwhelmed by the threat, feels an urgent need to do something about it.

It didn't happen overnight, but I've reached a point in my personal evolution where I think you simply have to confront things and call them out. Naturally, you still have to pick your battles, and there's no need to turn every tiff into an altercation. But if somebody's objective is to throw you in the garbage can, you have every right to stop that nonsense.

Bullying can look like a lot of things. Sure, someone could physically knock you over, but that same person could tell you to take it down a notch or invalidate something you're clearly good at. They could frantically intervene the very moment you start experiencing momentum or success. They could even use the moment of your happy expression—your smile, your laugh, your carefree emanation of joy—to burst your bubble by whatever means possible (physically/emotionally/mentally/all of the above). Worse, a bully can take it upon themselves to spoil the good and decent life you've carved out for yourself.

Bogged down by their own issues, these people may not even see themselves as bullies. And the energy they could be devoting to bettering themselves, overcoming their flaws, or—most critically—solidifying their own identity gets expended on lazy, destructive goals. They put others down to bring themselves up. They figure if you're lower, they'll be higher. But even if they manage to get you down and keep you there, soon enough another threat will appear on their radar, and the cycle will repeat.

That brings me to why it's important to call things out when we see them. Sherry, who liked to stuff me in the garbage can, got a huge lesson in her lack of power the day I fought back. Until then, she had presumed her advantage. Her leverage wasn't something she'd ever doubted. She went to bed at night secure in the knowledge that she could pick on me any time she chose. But when I fought back, she became a laughingstock. Suddenly, her minions proved disloyal; they were too desperate for someone to laugh at to be compassionate about their leader's downfall.

Had I not taken action and called out Sherry's wrongdoing, her presumption of power (in lieu of a real and valuable identity) would have remained intact. It's important to be mindful about not letting bullies get too comfortable in their assumptions. This is delicate work—we don't want to start finding bullies everywhere we look and feel the need to knock down any semblance of power or privilege whenever we see it (which would make *us* the bullies). But when people work overtime to frame our gains, successes, pluses, virtues, and wins as anything but, we know we're dealing with a bully, and we have a responsibility to call them out.

With a posse in our corner to protect us, this becomes much easier. And if calling out has to go beyond the shedding of light and into other forms of justice or self-protection, then so be it. The bottom line is that the bully should not feel safe doing what they are doing. Take it back to Trump: he didn't win the presidency, he got away with it. Remember when Michelle Obama said, "When they go low, we go high"?

Well, either we didn't go high enough . . . or we didn't go low enough. Either way, in the end, the bully kept perceiving himself as anything but.

Hiding behind fake names and online anonymity makes online trolls feel emboldened to mess with other people. Like I said before, what was once an in-the-field practice can now be done from the comfort of an armchair. But there's another force at work around online bullying, one a bit subtler yet perhaps equally important: now, more than ever, people can see what everybody else has—at least people's polished, controlled, hyper-positive presentations of it.

This, for bullies, is a waking nightmare. Imagine having a weak identity yourself and being subjected daily to ultra-vivid, carefully edited social media profiles in which other people's identities appear solid, confident, and unassailable. You're going to have to do something about this, aren't you?

Social media not only lets people edit out their flaws, but they can edit out their failures too. Even those who own up to them online can package, polish, and control the manner in which they do so, saving face by minimizing all the times they've been made to feel like weak, ineffectual, idiotic, garden-variety failures. This is no good for the perceptual fields of bullies, who aren't out there trying their own hands at success and are ill-acquainted with how that goes hand in hand with failure—you can't have one without the other. All day long, we're rewiring our psyches by editing out the failures, front-loading the successes, collecting likes and acclaim—and outraging the trolls in the process.

Meanwhile, clinching success goes beyond having to experience failure first. In actuality, the process is more nuanced than that. Not only do you have to fail before you succeed, but you have to do something arguably way harder and more humbling: you have to *learn* from your failures. That's deep work. It forces you to admit that the way you saw and did things before wasn't working. The only path to surviving and thriving is doing things differently . . . and knowing that as you do those things, you might find yourself failing all over again.

Bullies are not involved in this game. Self-reflection, making adjustments, trying and trying until they succeed—it's all too hard, and certainly harder than just pooping on someone else who's doing it. In fact, I call trolling the "snoop and poop." You snoop around and gain some shallow surface information, you feel your whole worldview shake, and you take a nice, big poop on whoever made you so upset.

If you act like this for long enough, your mind becomes so caked with negativity that you lose all reasonable perspective. The last thing it would occur to you to utter is, "Hey, I don't have all the answers." No, you wouldn't be caught dead saying that, because you're way too high on your own endless stream of criticism toward others. That false power has downright intoxicated you, which is a shame because one of the best parts of life is being open and receptive to other people's perspectives.

Here's what we have to teach our children: Diverse perspectives matter. Not only that, but they allow more growth with the flow!

People commonly confuse diversity for politics, but this is really a matter of sheer human survival. We can't navigate life's complexities—from school to the workplace to our own homes—without being open to other people's perspectives. Those perspectives will consistently surprise us. They'll shed light on angles we were either ignoring or had never imagined. Sometimes we'll deem those alternative perspectives useless. Much of the time, though, if we're humble, we'll come to understand that life offers no finer teacher than other people.

Bullies would rather not be taught by other people; their need for control is too great. If we're honest with ourselves, we all have that irritable side that maintains a zero-tolerance position against other people's thoughts. Sometimes, our own voices are enough to deal with, and others' voices are thus unwelcome—nuisance at best, nightmare at worst. This is why it's so important that people learn to be open to outside perspectives when they're young. It's the key not only to being a high-functioning person, but to avoiding the trap of becoming a bully, a troll, a critic, or what have you.

After all, we want to always move forward, not get stuck in the mud. Failure is one form of feedback, and believe me, it is guaranteed. But verbal feedback—the stuff we get from actual people—is equally valuable for shaping who we are, and it's usually far less jarring than failure.

When you become receptive to other people's perspectives, you not only develop a deep inner peace around alternative thought processes, but you enter a whole new frontier of bravery: you become courageous enough to ask what other people think. Imagine that, asking for feedback. Not only being open, but actually opening the door. Doing this advances us as players in the game of life by developing an essential life skill: the ability to consistently reinvent ourselves.

After all, we want to always move forward, not get stuck in the mud. Failure is one form of feedback, and believe me, it is guaranteed. But verbal feedback—the stuff we get from actual people—is equally valuable for shaping who we are, and it's usually far less jarring than failure.

Feedback is uncomfortable, sure. We'd be lying if we said we *loved* it, especially if we're smart, because smart people tend to think we already have it covered. So when feedback comes along, we might throw up a wall of resistance and invalidate, dismiss, or ignore the new information. Big mistake.

Successful people are skilled at reinventing themselves. They know the same old, same old doesn't cut it. They know the reinvention process should probably happen with far more frequency than one might imagine. It should be ongoing, constantly adding new layers, angles, attitudes, styles, information, and insights. Growing with the times, the trends, the changes. Growing with the flow.

Bullies, in the context of our grow-with-the-flow metaphor, are sharks in the water. The more you swim, the more sharks you'll encounter. Some will bite you, others will brush up against you, but the only way to avoid them is by staying onshore.

Bullies exist on a spectrum, from overtly hostile to passive-aggressive. The most obvious kind is the classic schoolyard or workplace meanie who tears you down with unmasked ferociousness. But online trolls are bullies too, as are people who simply trade in an excess of unwarranted criticism. Important safety tip: Never confuse valuable feedback with basic, bald criticism. The former is nuanced and can be positive, negative, or neutral. The latter is just constantly negative.

Putting behavior on a spectrum invites controversy, of course. In the #MeToo movement (which is intensely applicable here, as those who perpetuate sexual misconduct are certainly bullies too), stories about rape appear alongside stories of groping, verbal harassment, or awkward dates. Men cry, "Don't conflate rape with an awkward date!" Women cry back, "But it's all part of a greater pattern!" Likewise, when I say a critic is a troll is a bully, pushback is inevitable. Somebody who deems themselves a bit critical might protest, "Hey, I may be judgmental, but I'm not out to make anyone's life a living hell."

But consider how this behavior can escalate. What I haven't yet mentioned is the category of extreme bullies who validate my use of the word "shark" in this chapter. I'm talking about those who kill people. Time and time again, in this frightening age of mass shootings, we'll come to learn that somebody who's carried out a mass shooting was previously an online troll. It's illuminating, but it shouldn't be surprising, and the link validates the spectrum.

Of course, there's a difference between a mosquito bite and a lion attack. On the other hand, both creatures want blood. When it comes to bullies, the underlying principles are equally cohesive: weak identity + envy + entitlement + dehumanized insensitivity = bully. That's the nature of the shark.

As you grow with the flow, you'll find sharks in the water. Swimming with a posse of friendly fish and setting boundaries will help send out a warning signal that if a shark comes near, they won't have an easy time of it. Meanwhile, when one does come close, never forget that evasion is not a catch-all solution. Sometimes, yes, evading is effective. Oftentimes, though, you're better off putting up a fight.

That way, when the shark swims back to their friends, frowning and bruised, they will be sending a message, far and wide, that you are not a fish to mess with. Then you can swim on with pride, knowing that although other battles await you, the one you just won has only made you stronger.

Chapter Seven

THE ILLUSION OF CONTROL

"With every experience, you alone are
painting your own canvas, thought
by thought, choice by choice."

—OPRAH WINFREY

In 2018, our first Christmas home after Hurricane
Harvey was drawing near. Thanksgiving had passed.
We were home, but the end of the year typically invites speculation about the future, especially in the
energy business. Companies always seem to carry out
layoffs before the year's end, and that year, rumors
were circulating that the energy services companies
were taking another round.

We're told that working hard will always pave the
way. There's an unspoken, sacred pact between the
effort we put in and the results we get back . . . isn't
there? If we're totally honest with ourselves, we know
there isn't. We wish life could be like an arcade game,

where dropping in a few more quarters will always gain us more rounds, but the cause and effect doesn't work out nearly that clean. If you doubt this, you need only to experience that waiting period before you find out whether you're getting laid off. You've put in the work, you've been valuable, you've been sincere—but in the end, it's all going to come down to dollars and cents.

That year, as we waited, I got to thinking about a topic that's of huge importance to everyone, but that tends to fly below our radar: how much we control. When Harvey rolled his way up my street—into my neighborhood, my home, my life, my sanity—he taught me a massive lesson about control, namely that human beings have virtually none. The good news is, we get to spend a lot of our lives ignoring this fact. Oh, we're good at compartmentalizing— taking things piece by piece, day by day, hour by hour. Accordingly, we often grant ourselves the illusion of control. We say to ourselves, "Just get through today. Get through this morning. Get through the next five minutes." It's not control, but it bears some semblance of it. Our minds are brilliant at framing reality and granting coherency to chaos. But when we take a dangerous peek around that facade, we come to realize we control nothing.

Job-wise, it doesn't matter if you're self-employed or if you have a boss. The former will grant you expanded margins of flexibility, but you'll still have your company and your clients and your marketplace to answer to. You might think you're your own boss, but believe me, reality knows everything about being the boss of you. No matter what we do to enhance our perception that we have control, the hands of fate are always locked around the steering wheel.

So where's the good news in all this madness? It's simple, though harder than it sounds. The truth is, we do control two things: 1) our thoughts and 2) how we respond to crises.

OUR THOUGHTS

Nothing is more personal, more private, than our thoughts. Nothing in the world can be more validly labeled our property, our terrain, than our thoughts and the landscape upon which they dance. Everyone has this in common. Yes, some of us think more originally than others, and many of our thoughts are copies of someone else's. Some people are so afraid of thinking for themselves that they'll use any means—booze, drugs, TV, food, constant companionship—to avoid it.

But your thoughts are who you are, and that makes them sacred. They're your purest property, alongside your body, which is just a vehicle for your abstract thoughts. Your thoughts are more elastic in their creativity. They grant you doorways to other worlds. And to the extent that we can control them, they give us some semblance of control over our lives.

To be sure, it'd be much better to be God and just control everything outright. The way we're built, all we can do is master our own inner terrain. This is easier for some than for others, depending on the state of their mental health; some people literally cannot control their thoughts. But I believe our power upon this sacred mental ground is infinite. It's all a matter of tapping it, honing it, nourishing it, and wielding it effectively.

Underlying your thoughts is your attitude. If you have trouble thinking positively, your attitude is the culprit. Even in the case of someone struggling with mental health obstacles, their attitude plays a gigantic role in their mind's tendencies, biases, patterns, and general drifts.

Check your attitude. Be realistic. If you're inclined toward optimism, you're fortunate; pessimism is a tougher nut to crack. Your attitude drives your worldview, which drives your thoughts, which, alongside the hands of fate, drives your entire life.

Now, be real: What life outcomes do you desire? Because you're reading this book, I'm going to guess you want positive ones, regardless of how positive or negative your day-to-day thoughts are. Knowing your desired outcomes is powerful, as it clarifies how you want your thoughts to look on an ongoing basis.

It's important, for example, not to frame your desired outcomes as far-off fantasies you don't deserve. Feeling that way means you're questioning your own self-worth. Go easy on yourself. It doesn't matter what you've done, what mistakes you've made, who you've been in the past, or what you're most afraid of. Like anyone else, you deserve a shot at happiness.

Getting over this mindset begins—where else—in your thoughts. You have to come to a place where you self-identify not as the limited person who has these troubling thoughts, but as the infinitely powerful person who identifies with your ideal outcome. Are you hearing me? The bad thoughts aren't you; the desired outcome is. Every day, remind yourself of this. You're not too weak to think positively; you're strong enough to see with clarity the positive results you desire and deserve. Once you align yourself to those results, you'll quickly see that they aren't an endgame after all. They're your nature, your essence, your attitude. Honor your utmost vision of yourself to cultivate a version of you that reflects and embodies your vision in reality. Your thoughts *can* reshape reality. It's freaking magic.

Look around at how the successful people you admire are doing, attitude-wise. With the same metric, look at how the unsuccessful people are doing. The successful ones certainly have their problems—everybody does—but they're unlikely to be bitter, resentful, or scared. That doesn't mean every successful person has the same worldview as Mary Poppins, but it does mean they have some degree of control over their thoughts, and can steer them, and their lives in general, in a positive direction.

Our inner worlds are sacred not just because they're our deep, intimate, personal property, but because they are the mechanism by which we can define our outer worlds.

This brings us to the second thing we can control.

OUR RESPONSES TO CRISES

Once we've optimized our inner worlds, honing our minds into sharp, heat-seeking missiles of positive thought, we can get to work pulling off the ultimate power grab: responding to crises in a constructive and empowered way.

This is only possible with a positive mind. A negative mind is never ready for a crisis; indeed, a crisis only confirms our already-stewing negative biases. But a positive mind stands ready to counter and adapt to anything. I know, crises are unpredictable. We never have any notion as to what form, scale, or level of intensity they will be. Worst of all, we don't know when they will end.

We can battle them with real mental strength, however. Again, keep your eye on your desired positive outcomes. Make those your identity. Make that stuff the place where your mind and heart always dwell. It's like building a muscle: the more you exercise your positive thinking, the more naturally it will come to you. Then, even the nastiest crisis, painful as it may be, will not be able to yank out your deeply positive mental roots.

It all comes down to the mind-body connection. Just as a healthy body can't be toppled by a single cigarette or a greasy cheeseburger, a healthy mind stands ready to confront all kinds of crises. The more positive your mind is, the less you'll even perceive crises as such when they arise. You might look like a happy idiot in that scenario, but in reality, you're just attuned to the fact that everything has an upside, a silver lining, or an opportunity for growth. Your mind will be so sculpted around positive thinking that when negativity interferes, you will be unable to forget that within that negativity is enormous potential for positivity. Don't take my word for it; just try it.

It's one thing to have a positive attitude or disposition. It's another thing to cultivate positive thinking as though your life depends on it—because it does.

The better your attitude and outlook, the better your life. It's not just a simple matter of perception, either; it's actual quantum physics. Quantum science has proven that the perceiving party and the perceived thing are one united entity, carrying out a complex routine, such that everything we're experiencing is deeply influenced by the fact that *we're* the ones experiencing it.

This isn't about placing blame. I'm not saying all the bad things that happen to you are your own doing. If somebody told me that I caused Hurricane Harvey, I'd have a few choice words for them. At a quantum level, however, what we experience is in a fundamental union with our faculties of perception. That means we can bend and shape reality—literally, not just in terms of what lens we view it through. We collaborate with reality through our actions; the things we do and the choices we make bring about tangible, real-world results. The collaboration is so intense that reality is dependent on our view of it in order to continue existing.

Check it out: You, a positive person, have conditioned your mind to favor the upsides of all things. Then along comes a storm, and you, also an imperfect human, get scared and panic. But what you don't do is fold. You don't stop fighting back or fail to come up with productive ideas. You don't let the storm make you its bitch.

Instead, you practice basic resilience. That storm—literally or metaphorically—is now your collaborator. You didn't invite it to the party, and you could certainly do without its presence, but here it is, doing its thing. You can't walk away; it's leading a conga line *all around* you. Going along with it becomes your only choice. So you dance your heart out.

> **Again, keep your eye on your desired positive outcomes. Make those your identity. Make that stuff the place where your mind and heart always dwell. It's like building a muscle: the more you exercise your positive thinking, the more naturally it will come to you.**

Before long, it dawns on you that even though you didn't invite the storm to the party, it actually wasn't the worst guest. Sure, you don't like it, and you hate what it's done to you, but, oh my, what a ball you had. Look what you did. Look what you learned. Look how you got to see yourself: positive, responsive, proactive, productive, resilient, surviving. In the end, the ultimate reward is a sweetness far deeper than survival itself. When we survive, we get the pride of knowing we're survivors.

Back to 2018, when our first Christmas post-Harvey was looming. At last, we got the news that Mark's job was safe. I looked around my house. It was still so new, a living reminder of the one we lost. But it was a real home nonetheless.

Our anticipation of Mark's potential layoff had been but another storm. Not a big one, nor a long one—just a storm, like so many others. It came, it went, and we survived. And as it happened, I noticed something: It didn't break us. It didn't crush us. It didn't make us fold. We got up the following morning and pressed on.

As you grow with the flow, see yourself as a captain, steering a ship upon the sea. Naturally, the weather will vary. As much as you hope for smoothness, you know your boat will rock. The weather is bound to shift. Storms are bound to test your skill. The thing is, you're not some flunky; you're the captain. You've prepared for this. You know how to navigate. Life and experience have honed you.

Being negative isn't even an option; only novices and amateurs, those unfamiliar with the sea and the transience of storms, embrace negativity. Those people are less acquainted with the beauty of clear, blue skies. You, though, are a badass captain, and most storms will not stop you. Indeed, you've come to see storms not as end points, but as transition points. They're temporary. They come and go. In the end, the majority of the time, a storm will simply clear the air, granting you clarity and momentum as you sail on, smiling, to whatever is next.

Chapter Eight

"I'M NOT READY"

"Standing in the middle of the road
is very dangerous; you get knocked
down by the traffic from both sides."

—MARGARET THATCHER

Speaking of our perceptions of control, think about how often you confront a challenge by saying, "I'm not ready." Here's a secret, one I've learned the hard way, and one I still need to remind myself of: those three words are useless. Note that I'm not saying they are false. Quite the contrary, they're always true—no one is ever ready. But just because they're true doesn't mean they're useful.

Say you're trying to do something big, like starting a business. It probably ties up your heart center, and it more than likely makes you a wee bit nervous, but you're focused on your noble ambitions. And then you look at all that's needed to start the business. It's a long list: financial steps, strategic steps, legal steps, marketing steps, and so on. When you see all those steps, you come to a fork in the road, and you hear yourself say, "I'm not ready."

Of course you're not! The road is long and tangled. The outcomes are unclear or unknown. Who has the time and energy for that? So you park your car at "I'm not ready," because it's the truth and nobody can tell you otherwise.

But then the oddest thing happens. First it's unsettling, then it's downright devastating. You look out the window and see the seasons are changing. The world is passing you by. You're losing time—one year, then two, then more years than you care to count. And guess what happened during all that time? You never managed to get ready.

Somehow, what was true before is still true now. You avoided a treacherous path because you were smart enough to know you weren't ready. Yet, in the end, that avoidance failed to solve your problem. Readiness never arrived. You're still stuck, unready, at square one, and you know that if you continue embracing this truth, you'll never get around to being ready. What a paradox.

Nobody in the world, in any field, at any point in history, is ever ready. But one group of people regularly fools us into thinking they are. It's a large and organized group, and its members are excellent at slinging convincing illusions of their effectiveness. I like to refer to this group as Other People.

Other people always look ready, don't they? Other people look on the ball, like they know what they're doing, they know their stuff, they've been up all night preparing. Obviously, I don't mean *all* other people. To be sure, lots of people look outright foolish. They don't inspire our confidence. But these people aren't nearly as distracting as those folks around us who just always look ready.

President Barack Obama, for example, always looked ready, carrying himself with utter confidence. But let me tell you something true, albeit unverified by research or science: even he wasn't ready. How do I know? Because Obama is a human being, and all human beings do something daily that we don't always admit to, even though it defines the very core of our humanity. Human beings improvise.

Life is one big, ongoing improv skit. Granted, it's not always as funny as *Saturday Night Live*, but most of what we do is made up on the fly. This doesn't mean you shouldn't do your homework or prepare. But even so, you will never truly find yourself ready because of reality's unpredictable nature.

I'm not about to pretend to dish all the universe's big secrets. Life's inner mechanisms are just as mysterious to me as they are to the next guy. However, I'm going to go out on a limb and propose something about the way human reality works, though we regularly lose sight of it: we are constantly faced with problems we weren't expecting.

Aren't life's train wrecks, trials, and storms always the things we weren't thinking about beforehand? If we were, then life wouldn't be very lifelike. I'm not saying we can't ever see storms coming on the horizon; sometimes we can. Ask anybody who's ever lived unhealthily and eventually had a heart attack. Case closed. Then again, that person didn't foresee the heart attack's timing or circumstances, nor the ensuing medication, bills, and so on.

> **Life is one big, ongoing improv skit. Granted, it's not always as funny as *Saturday Night Live*, but most of what we do is made up on the fly. This doesn't mean you shouldn't do your homework or prepare. But even so, you will never truly find yourself ready because of reality's unpredictable nature.**

The human system is built upon a foundation of unpredictability, and the nature of the problems we face is ever-changing. Problems are things of novelty;

if we knew how to solve them when they first arose, they wouldn't be problems. They'd be nothing, and we wouldn't even think about them. But even when we know a lot, and our education and experience have loaded us with wisdom and solutions, problems will always find a way to surprise us. That's just the way the life machine is rigged.

Knowing this, there's underlying support beneath my previous two points: 1) Other people always seem more prepared than we do, and 2) everything is just improv. Other people seem more prepared than we do because their problems aren't our problems. Have you ever been around someone who is sick or terminally ill and come away perceiving them as strong? Often, people in these circumstances don't perceive themselves that way—outsiders only do because they don't have the same problem. Outsiders can barely witness their pain, much less feel it. Other people look more together than we do because we don't have the burden of being them. We have the privilege of looking at them from the outside in, dealing with our own problems in the meantime.

Other people, who exist without the weight and depth of being you, display the illusion that they have it together. That's why people often fear public speaking; the audience seems more together, less vulnerable to mistakes, than they are. The speaker can try to assure themselves that the audience has just as many problems as they do, but that exercise in logic will not necessarily penetrate the illusion that the big, scary audience is filled with people who have their stuff together and know exactly what they're doing all the time.

This is such a commonplace illusion that it almost seems real, as though all of us are living in some warped, wild state of misunderstanding. Which we are. Even when you're studied up, experienced, the freaking best, you cannot be comprehensively ready for life's unpredictable variables all the time.

Which brings me back to the whole improv thing. That's how this works. If you can't be flexible and improvise, you're not going to be much of an asset to your team, company, family, or partner. Your ability to think on your feet and generate creative solutions to sudden problems might be your most valuable survival tool.

So the question isn't whether you're ready. The question is, are you ready to improvise? If you're stuck on those three foolish words—"I'm not ready"—what you're really saying is, "I'm not ready to improvise."

Improvising is frightening. It's walking on a tightrope, facing the mean, raw ferocity of each new day. It's about growing with the flow. But improv is what separates women from girls and boys from men. If you're the type who gets thrown off because everything's not going according to plan, then your deficiency isn't being unready, but being unable to bear that you'll never be ready.

Spontaneity is the taboo secret ingredient of success in every aspect of life. Spontaneity gets a bad reputation as the trait we ascribe to our too-cool friends, the ones who are dangerous and can't save money or plan ahead. But spontaneity is essential to our well-being. No living state is closer to death than freezing up because our waking reality does not match our previous expectations. People afraid of their unreadiness too often get stranded in this territory. They're attached to the idea of things looking, feeling, and functioning a certain way, and in so doing, they let the mystifying beauty of real life pass them by.

Picture a dance floor. The people dancing are no more ready than the ones sitting in their seats. The difference is that the ones dancing have embraced the life-fueling principle of spontaneity. They don't know what song is coming next. They don't know what moves they'll do. They may not even know who, if anyone, will join them, but at least they're out there doing it.

Meanwhile, the ones on the sidelines just . . . don't feel ready. Sure, they're warming up to it—waiting for the right moment, the right feeling, the right song . . . if it comes. But they shouldn't be waiting for it. They should just get out there already. Because once you're out there, life starts happening. Stuff gets real.

You'll have strange encounters. You'll surprise yourself. In fact, the surprises won't ever cease. But at least you'll have cracked the code to this whole readiness thing, because you will have at last gone out there, ready or not.

"Carpe the chaos," Gloria Feldt, a wise woman and friend, once said. I treasure those words (which, by the way, are way better than "I'm not ready"). Life *is* chaos. I wish it felt more stable, and I could just have one day where every single thing went as planned. Maybe if I'd decided to try to avoid life, things would be more predictable. If I, say, just spent my life eating or watching television or playing video games, I'm sure each day would wonderfully resemble the one before and after it.

But that's not life; that's a slow death. Besides, even in the cage of our own self-imposed stasis, problems and challenges will always manage to find their way to us. Like I said, that's just how this whole system is designed.

"Carpe the chaos," or "Seize the chaos," is a way of framing your whole life as a choice. Do you choose to be active or passive, to take control or relinquish it? Do you choose to dance or miss out on the fun?

The bottom line is that it's always a choice. Hurricane Harvey shoved that reality right in my face. That storm helped me sort the trivial from the truly important. If I learned anything from living through it, it was that every day presents an invaluable opportunity to move forward, because you're as ready as you'll ever be.

> **Improvising is frightening. It's walking on a tightrope, facing the mean, raw ferocity of each new day. It's about growing with the flow. But improv is what separates women from girls and boys from men.**

As the icing on that cake, that means nobody on this strange blue planet is even a little bit more ready than you are. Sure, we all have our differing devotions and disciplines, and we might all be at different stages of progress, but at the end of the day, readiness is all a state of mind.

If you're ready, you're ready. If you're not ready, you're ready. And if you're ready, you're not ready. It's all an illusion, a choice we make—either seizing the chaos, or letting it consume us. Life is short, and it goes fast.

Chaos: I am ready to seize you.

Chapter Nine

THE THREE TRAITS YOU NEED TO SUCCEED

"Vision, will, and grit. Rinse and repeat."

—KATIE MEHNERT

On Saturday mornings, I slow run. Oftentimes, that clears my head. Sometimes, it's just overwhelming. Either way, I wish I made more space to run. Running requires a success mentality—you have to get where you're going, and you have to finish what you started. I used to regularly run marathons, but my business schedule interrupted that pattern. Too bad, especially when Texas weather climbs above eighty degrees. You're out there running, lungs working overtime, sweating like you're in a sauna . . . and then you start to think.

The idea for this chapter came to me during a run, when I got to thinking about success. The exercise was taxing, and I couldn't stand it at times. Yet some immense, primal force insisted I keep at it. What does it take? What was fueling me to keep my body in motion toward success? Vision, will, and grit, I decided.

1. VISION

Success requires a vision, a clear sense of where you're going. The clearer your target is, the better your chance of reaching it.

A lot of people get thrown when it comes to narrowing down their vision. Even smart people can get tripped up because they are multitalented enough to rise to many occasions. These people might be better at someone else's job than that person is, even though it isn't their specialty.

Well, cool it with the back-patting, smart-ass. Even though you're smart as a whip, you might be struggling to lock in on a clear vision of who and what you want to be, or exactly what you wish to succeed at. That's why your vision is worthy of work. Tune in and get real. Ask yourself what your most fundamental truth is—what you love the most, where you rise the highest, where you run the fastest, where you offer the most value. What do you want to be remembered for when you are gone? If many answers show up, you deserve props, but don't be surprised when a bunch of divergent, messy avenues crop up in your path. Reality is a mirror; it will always show you what you are.

So get sharp about it. It's just like with running, when you have an end point in mind. If you're running to the marsh, for example, you're not thinking, "Well, I may stop at the marsh or I may stop at the store or I may curve around to the school." No, you're set on the marsh, your goal and vision. You're not going to subject yourself to useless inner noise. As such, your path is clear.

Naturally, obstructions will come. Maybe along Cedar Avenue, a truck will block your path and you'll have to curve around it. Or maybe the obstruction runs deeper and the marsh is closed, so you have to revise your vision. When that happens, it's okay. The important thing is that you're clear about your initial vision, so that if and when it needs to be replaced, you're in a state of mind where lining up an equally clear replacement comes easily.

The only wrong thing you can do in this scenario— even worse than being unclear about your vision—is go out there with no vision whatsoever. You can't just fall backwards into life blindfolded, thinking, "Something will catch me." Although I applaud you for your Zen tranquility, the non-vision approach to success will result in something even more troubling than a confusing path: no path at all. People who know you won't think much of you. You'll have no specialty. You'll be unfocused. You'll get a reputation, no matter how smart you are, for being a zero. "Oh, Shelly? Yeah, she's just . . . kind of there." Shrug!

> **A vision not only grants you clarity and momentum, but it also grants you an identity. Your vision will become who you are and how people know you. Your vision is one and the same as your reputation, and it will happen no matter where you are in relation to your goal.**

Don't walk around being a living, human shrug. A vision not only grants you clarity and momentum, but it also grants you an identity. Your vision will become who you are and how people know you. Your vision is one and the same as your reputation, and it will happen no matter where you are in relation to your goal. Whether you're at the starting line or at the finish line, people will say, "Oh, Amanda's into dentistry." But the social component is far less meaningful than the truth component. Your vision must be a pure expression of who you are, what you want, and what lights you up.

Like I said in chapter 2, I wrote my vision for Pink

Petro and Experience Energy down on an airplane cocktail napkin. The vision was big, but the napkin was small, which forced me into sharply defining my terms. I saw a gap where women were underrepresented in my industry. It was an opportunity to create a company to empower and motivate women and minorities in the energy field to make up the next generations of leaders and solve big, hairy challenges. I clearly saw that we needed a way to engage everyone in the new energy economy, but more importantly, I felt called to this vision. I felt like the one who could make it happen, that the vision in my mind and the person I am were tightly aligned.

Your vision has to be the same. This is not to say the path from cocktail napkin to reality was smooth. A strong vision shouldn't be mistaken for a cruise down Easy Street. But the clearer your vision and the more imbued it is with your fundamental truths and strengths, the less of a struggle your path to success will be. In fact, if it's *all* struggle—if you're constantly pushing a boulder up a hill—then I hate to break it to you, but you're on the wrong path. It's hard to admit, I know. You might even feel a deep love for what you're going after, but it's misaligned with who you are and what you have to offer.

I spent years working in corporate environments, rising up in the ranks. But throughout all that time, I never felt like I totally fit in anywhere. And I didn't—I often moved around from here to there. As it turned out, that entire time, I was just an entrepreneur and didn't even know it yet. It wasn't that I couldn't take orders, follow directions, or work on teams—I made it all happen. But I always felt that my head was out of proportion to the jobs I was in. I was always looking to innovate, fill gaps, push things ahead, and make new music. In time, I realized the best way to do that was on my own.

Let's bring it back to running. What are you doing out there on a steep hill if it's making you feel like you're about to have a heart attack? Clearly, you're not aligned to the dumb hill—you need some fresh terrain. Your run should be challenging and should whip you into shape, but that doesn't mean it has to kill you.

Think of what your friends would say if you walked in the door, all bruised and heaving, saying, "Oh, man, I just ran up this steep hill!" Your friends would know right away that hill is not for you. Maybe later, sure, but not right now. That's what's annoying about other people: they often have a clearer sense of who we are and where we fit than we do. Sometimes, their feedback will shatter our own self-perceptions and we'll respond self-righteously, defending our choice to run up steep hills. Sometimes, we're even right about it. Screw them—don't tell me where to run!

The key is to get in touch with our truth, to clear out all the illusions. That's how you parse wise advice from lazy naysaying. What is the sheer truth of what we can offer? Where does our value lie? Where do we rise the highest? Where can we maximize our current potential?

Brush your ego aside too—it's what wants us to brave the hill. Your ego wants the hype of applause more than the quiet contentment of making meaningful contributions. Over the long run, the applause won't matter. We'll want to be sure we left this world better than we found it. The only way you brave those trails is by going in with a vision.

2. WILL

Where does will come from? It's a mysterious thing. It's especially mysterious in the course of running. There you are with these two legs carrying you along, and you're like, "Where am I getting the fuel to keep on going?"

Will is fuel. Some people say it feels like a fire in your belly. And if you're ambitious, you can bet it never lets up. Like Bruce Springsteen said, you have a fire in the hole that just won't quit.

What starts the fire? I once wondered if will wasn't in the same category as talent—perhaps it can be nurtured like a plant, but if it ain't there, then it ain't there. I no longer believe that's the case with will, however. I believe everyone has it; it's part of nature's design. It propels us out of the birth canal. It helps us crawl and walk. Will even powers our bodies' passive systems as, over time, we grow: bones, teeth, hair. We're machines in motion, sprouting newness and activity. But during most of our time on Earth, by design, we can strive, flow, rise, prosper, and accomplish. All that requires will.

So, what gets our will going? One simple word: love. Our will is directly proportional to our level of love. That's why I hammered the point about our vision being truthful. If we're not acting from truth, we're not acting from love. In fact, being truthful is one of the most loving things you can do in the world, for both yourself and others. Sure, your truth may not be the whole truth or everybody else's truth, but it represents your essence, and as such, it has major value. Expressing your essence—so long as you're not hurting anybody or yourself—is a bold, beautiful act of love. In fact, the more you align to your truth, and the more you live and express yourself from a state of love, the more willpower you have.

Let's bring it back to running. Previously, our destination was a simple place; all we needed was a vision. Now, we're going deeper and progressing from a place of love. If we don't, we have no will.

Let's switch out the destination and say you're

running to the love of your life. Your knight in shining armor awaits you. They are standing on a street corner, checking their watch. Your job is to run to them, so you run faster, harder. You'll move heaven and Earth to get there. You're a woman (or a man) on fire. You, in other words, have been blessed with willpower.

Will exists in proportion to what you're willing yourself toward. It all comes down to your basic priorities. Health-oriented people are more mindful—more willful—about keeping up good hygiene and eating well than those who are less mindful about their well-being. Those who are money-oriented will always find the motivation to move in the direction of money.

Those of us who become parents learn a great deal about will and the loving energy that fires it up. We realize we're capable of waking up at all hours and tapping our deep well of will to look after this little person we love so much. We realize we'll go to extremes to attend to, nurture, coddle, respect, talk to, and overall love this little human being.

If will is fuel, then love is the engine it powers. It's essential to do something you love, as that love will not only arm your life with meaning, but it'll provide willpower as a wondrous element of the overall package. Once you have will, you're unstoppable, baby. People will see it and know what they're dealing with.

They'll be like, "This one's coming and—nope! She ain't stopping."

Without will, there is no success. As you progress toward your vision, you'll be challenged repeatedly with strange, new, and daunting prospects. Will is your best buddy as you confront them. Without will, you back down or crap out. You need will to be successful in this world.

> **Once you have will, you're unstoppable, baby. People will see it and know what they're dealing with. They'll be like, "This one's coming and—nope! She ain't stopping."**

Yeah, you can fake it until you make it, especially when you're young. You can tap your own God-given energy and apply it to tasks that you only half care about, but that won't work forever. One day, you'll find yourself burned out. Burnout is what happens when you put in energy and don't receive proportional energy back—your hard work is not justly rewarded. You may even get burned out doing things you love, things that won't always produce rewards. But at least, because you love them, they'll boost your will. Half the time, you won't even notice the boost. You'll just do what you gotta do. It'll be a love thing, the mark of your commitment. The more you love what you're doing, the more committed you'll be. Love = commitment = will.

With vision and will, you need one final component to make yourself unstoppable: grit.

3. GRIT

In general, we think of grit as toughness. Toughness is generally perceived from the outside: the steely gaze, the upright spine, the take-no-BS attitude. But what does toughness—grit—look like from the inside?

Grit is the ability to tune out the noise. When you're successful, or even in pursuit of success, you're going to be exposed to lots of noise—the doubters, the haters, the naysayers, the coattail-riders, the unsolicited advisers, the competitors, and the marketplace itself: customers, prospects, clients, vendors.

Success is noisy because it's inherently social, just like humans ourselves. Success does not exist in a bubble. In fact, if you're the type who fantasizes about someday disappearing into a fortress, and thus insulating yourself from the cold, hard, loud world, more power to you—but the day you disappear into that fortress is the day your success begins to erode. I don't care if you have millions in the bank. You have to stay in the scene and keep your ear to the ground. You need to exist within the flow of information and innovation. You need, in other words, to be a social creature, and that means you're going to be exposed to noise.

The noise is distracting. People will get under your skin and—forcefully or otherwise—take command of your emotions. You'll lose whole days, maybe even months, processing the fallout of something somebody said.

The only way to manage the noise is to up your grit. With grit, you're like a boulder in the storm. Whereas everything else is getting blown around, you're planted in one spot. You'll be the one who takes things with a grain of salt. You're not a reactor; you *create* the reactions. You're the noisemaker, not the noise taker. The rainmaker, not the one who's soaking wet.

We all probably want to be steely, gritty, and tough. How in the world do we get there? It takes experience. But when I say experience equals grit, I don't mean that you'll ever get used to the noise, because you won't. The noise keeps changing, the voices keep shifting, and the information keeps updating. Experiencing the noise doesn't allow you to stop hearing it, but it does allow you to put the noise in perspective.

This is all about volume—not in terms of sound, but in terms of size. Throughout your success journey, you'll amass more and more human encounters.

People are far more diverse than we think, and they'll keep surprising you with the nature of their psyches, their perspectives, their positions. Over time, you'll become accustomed to the variety, and the chatter won't be so distracting. You'll have developed a feel for the way things go. Sure, somebody betrayed, insulted, challenged, or confronted you along the way—been there, done that.

You grow accustomed, which is not to say you ever stop being sensitive. Everyone is sensitive. The goal is not to become inhuman. Even the toughest gal you know has layers of soft, gooey emotion inside. That's the way our species was manufactured, much as we try to deny it. Grit, however, makes you less sensitive. It makes your hard, steely surface resemble your inner state. In other words, you're not faking it anymore. In the early days, your grit will be a front and you'll *have to* fake it until you make it. But as time goes on, people will see in your eyes the incomparable glare of someone who's been around.

Be gentle with yourself. This takes time—years. Be mindful on this point: if you're ten years into the game and still overreacting, that's on you, not the game. You're human and you deserve to be sensitive, but there's such a thing as being too sensitive. When you're reacting to the noise too much, you're draining emotional energy that could be better applied to kicking ass out in the world.

Perspective is the key. As the noise flares up and you find yourself reacting, take a step back. Look at your own back catalog and check out all the fires you've already put out. Then ask yourself if the current noise is worth your reaction. As time goes on, ideally, your perspective won't have to be consciously willed; you'll just have it and apply it. Such is the utmost beauty of perspective.

> **Grit is the ability to tune out the noise. When you're successful, or even in pursuit of success, you're going to be exposed to lots of noise—the doubters,the haters, the naysayers, the coattail-riders, the unsolicited advisers, the competitors, and the marketplace itself.**

As you develop and hone yours, be mindful of another form of noise that sneaks up on you. Most noises originate from other people, but don't forget the noise in your own head. That noise tells you that you're crazy, you suck, and you have unbreakable patterns, incurable hurts, and unclimbable walls. That kind of noise can cut right through your grit. Just like sensitivity, we all have it too. It's the voice that loves playing devil's advocate. Your whole plan is laid out, the horizon is well in view, then that devious little voice chimes in and blocks out the sun.

The technique for dealing with it is the same as above: perspective, perspective, perspective. Look that voice—that noise—right in the eye and ask, "Are you really here to help me?" The answer is almost always no.

So just move on. Sure, it'll keep on yapping, but it doesn't have to be the queen of you. It's just your natural shadow—the price we pay for throwing off so much light.

Vision, will, and grit work together in an interlocking fashion. Vision lays the foundation, sets the tone, and commands the outlook. Will allows you to navigate the territory. Grit allows you to survive and excel within the navigation process. But no discussion of success is complete without mention of its dreaded opposite: failure.

It will come as news to none of you that failure is absolutely necessary in the process of achieving success. Not only will you fail, but you will fail hard and repeatedly. Sometimes you'll spend years in failure mode. That's why vision, will, and grit are so important. They're your fortification, your ways of staying on point, in motion, and in your strength.

Failure brings to mind some pretty dramatic things, such as fortresses crumbling and us on the floor, head in our hands, in despair. But the everyday truth of failure is more subtle. For one thing, failure has a lot to do with hearing the word no. Failure is rejection, avenues going cold, doors being shut, people conveying that they don't wish to work with you or pick up what you're putting down. Failure is also marked by isolation. Sometimes we fail when no one stands with us. Sometimes failure comes down to not having allies or ending up with the wrong allies, who leave us stranded or worse off for their company.

Are you seeing how married to success vision, will, and grit are? The marriage is functional because vision, will, and grit chip away at failure. No failure in the world can kill your vision. Sure, a failure can modify it, but failure can't knock it off the face of the Earth. And if it does, the only one to blame is yourself because it wasn't the vision that got hurt, but your will. And if you were vulnerable to your will being rocked, it's because you didn't have the required grit.

When you have your vision-will-grit package under control, your whole relationship to failure changes. Not only are you calmer in the face of failure's inevitability, but you can pull off a pair of magic tricks that only successful people can master: failing faster and failing harder.

1. FAILING FASTER

Successful people are fast freaking failures. Who ever talks about rushing the process of failure? Believe me, you can rush it. Rush it on the front end, when the failure occurs, and rush it on the back end, when you're stewing in its icky aftermath.

Here's what successful people are good at, in terms of failing faster. First, we see failure coming on the horizon. We've already failed so much that we've developed a nose for the stuff. We have a strange sixth sense when a new coworker is not quite a fit. We have an inkling that this latest idea isn't going to fly. Call it intuition or psychic power, or just call it common sense.

When starting any new endeavor, we all have questions and hesitations. If we're human and smart, we have an eye on the downsides. Some downsides stand out more than others. These are the things we know could overturn our ship, but—before we get good at failing fast—we ignore them and just hope for the best.

For example, let's say you bring in a new partner. From the get-go, the partner seems envious—they drop little comments or compete too much with you. The partner has you under a microscope, but the partner is highly qualified, so you roll with it and see where it leads. And, yep, it leads to the exact same place as your last toxic relationship: hell. Everything goes south. Your partner is out to get you. Business is stalling. Your partner certainly isn't making anything better, so, months later, you finally cancel the whole thing.

Those who develop the skill to fail fast can eliminate the whole "months later" part from the progression. We may not even make the partnership decision to begin with. Like I said, it's just in the air; we know before we know. This doesn't mean you should be paranoid and burn every bridge before it's even built. But you need to trust that voice in your gut when it issues grave warnings. They won't come often, but they will come. Ignore them at your own risk.

On the back end of failing fast, in the partnership example, successful people don't take the rest of the year off when a situation knocks them down. We absorb and move on. We don't stew, linger, return to the scene of the crime, or obsess over all the threads of evidence. We fail fast, we make failure our bitch, and we do so because we are successful.

2. FAILING HARDER

As if failure isn't already hard enough, failing harder means committing to your failure. You go all in. You rub your own nose in it.

Why torture yourself? Well, you're trading short-term pain for long-term comfort. Let's say you launched a new product that flops. You had six successful product launches in a row, but this seventh one suddenly leaves your customers cold. It's an embarrassing setback. It leaves the brand reeling and leaves you eager for a comeback.

Get moving on that comeback! Like, yesterday. As I said before, fail faster. But don't fail so fast that you miss the failure's inherent usefulness. It has wisdom and lessons to offer you. Whereas you shouldn't obsess and linger at the scene of the crime, you should fail all the way and take everything from that failure that you can. If you miss the chance to do so, you're wandering right into the definition of insanity: doing the same thing over and over and expecting different results.

In the failed product example, let's say you don't fail hard enough and your ego gets in the way. You're critical of some minor aspects of the product, but willfully blind to its central flaws (the ones everybody else seems comfortable looking at straight on). So, six months later, you launch your eighth product, and it's just a mild upgrade of the seventh one, absent the vision, will, or grit to rip out those aspects that made it terrible. How's your business looking now, girl? Are you now known for being stubborn?

You have to fail harder next time. Wallow in the

full blow of failure. Let it leave a giant hole in you. It hurts, but because you're failing faster, you'll get on with life soon enough.

Don't be the one who doesn't get the lesson. When you fail, all you have left is the lesson. If you fail to get that, you fail completely. Sure, you didn't want the lesson. It's at odds with what you previously thought. But you can either be the person who evolves and adapts (grows with the flow) or the woman who gets stuck in a rut of her own making. I know which one I strive to be.

The whole vision-will-grit practice lends itself perfectly to the classic story of *The Wizard of Oz*. Dorothy had a vision: her first destination was the wizard; her ultimate destination was home. She had the will to dance down that yellow brick road. And she had the grit to manage the journey, despite the witch and flying monkeys who sought to ruin her.

In fact, Dorothy's journey is pretty much every woman's journey. We're all just trying to find our way, and while we're at it, we run into lots of dudes—dudes with no brains, heart, or courage. But the real kicker is Dorothy's encounter with Oz. He's not the great and powerful being he pretended to be. No, the guy is just a fraud—some lame dude behind a curtain.

It's all traumatic and disappointing, but in the end, courtesy of her vision, will, and grit, Dorothy gets to go someplace, the likes of which exist no place else: home.

It's a timeless story—although our vision contains our destiny, in the end it is home that matters. Our center, a place of family, safety, stability, warmth, and memories. Beyond all our other goals, that is what's at stake and what defines success above all else.

This is not to say we have to stay there. In fact, whenever we choose, we can recharge our vision and seek out the Emerald City once again.

Chapter Ten

DON'T SWEAT WHAT WASN'T MEANT TO BE

"Oh, come on. Life's too short.
Suck it up and move on!"

—HANNAH RUCKER

In the course of never being ready for anything at all, there's one thing we're seriously never ready for. Indeed, we dread it. We go out of our way to avoid it. Rejection.

Rejection is what happens when you want somebody but they don't want you back. When we're rejected, it seems like the entire human community wants nothing to do with us, as though our very species just can't bear its affiliation with us any longer. And although this happens in both social and professional contexts, I'm going to share one of my key professional rejection experiences. It ground up my soul, spat it out, and buried it deep underground.

Now, looking back, I thank my lucky stars that things turned out the way they did.

After that plane ride next to Bubba, I knew I had to build Pink Petro and Experience Energy. My idea was clear, the gap was open, and the need was undeniable. That didn't stop me from trying to sabotage myself, though, so after I left BP in 2014, I applied for a new job at Shell.

I'm ashamed to admit it. This little event has been taboo in my personal history, like that uncle you keep in the attic and try not to speak of very much. But truthfully, instead of building my business when I knew in my gut it was my calling, I attempted to get set up at Shell.

After I left BP, my cocktail napkins were with me every day, even in my sleep. But I also held this picture in my head of going back to Shell. In my mind, it was easy: just go back to the comfortable chair. Forget this whole "What would you do if you weren't afraid?" thing. I'd be working for an amazing woman there, and it was pretty much a done deal. I had to interview for it, but that was just a formality. This seat was open and waiting for me.

Until it wasn't. As it turned out, I'd misconstrued

the entire situation and underestimated my own fundamental need for independence at that juncture. That's not to say I suddenly got all philosophical when I didn't get the job. No, I freaked out. I couldn't believe it—how could they do this to me, let alone themselves? This rejection went down like sour medicine and sharp-edged stones. Not only did I have experience at Shell, but I had a solid network there. I was a badass! Why couldn't they remember that?

Here comes the happy ending. Not every rejection in our lives will lead to such a clean turnaround, but in this case, I came in for an awesome landing. Because when I started Pink Petro, guess who was my second-ever customer?

If you said Shell, you would be correct. Give yourself a prize!

Here's how it happened. When you align to your truth and tap into your passion, your passion refuses to leave you alone. It becomes almost like a stalker, only less terrifying and soul-sucking. Constantly, your passion starts knocking on all your doors. It wants in. In my case, Pink Petro and Experience Energy wouldn't leave me alone. This was a forced marriage, albeit one I was totally into. The courtship was rushed and jarring. The whole thing landed in my life like a spaceship in the backyard. I couldn't look away from it. It was hard to believe, but equally hard to ignore. I had to go build it.

Framing things this way—forced marriage, space-ship, knocking down doors—it makes sense that I'd run for cover at Shell. Who wants to deal with non-stop operatic bombast, especially when safer, calmer grounds are accessible? Well, such grounds weren't accessible to me—not anymore. The universe had thrown a steel door over them. It was wagging a finger in my face, saying, "Nuh-uh, Katie, this is not the deal." The deal was that I was being prepped for bigger things.

How about you? I have no doubt that you either want 1) bigger things or 2) to preserve, sustain, and/or enlarge the already big things you're rocking hard each day of your life. What is the key to that? Let's start with a simple metaphor: life is a door-lined hallway.

In life, you have to move and progress; you can't stand still. As we've established, standing still is the best way to miss out on life. So stay in motion, down the door-lined hallway, and take note of all those doors.

They're not just doors. Behind each one is an entire universe of possibilities. Each door leads to an experience, an adventure, a land of potential. Did I mention the hallway is extremely long, and the doors number in the trillions? That's what life is like: it's made of potential. As we grow older, we often forget this. We perceive our options as becoming limited.

We feel our bodies slowing down. We know our will is tangled up with our responsibilities. But the doors never diminish in number. There are plenty of them, lined up neatly on both sides of the hall, one after the other.

If we see life as limited, we can bet that's exactly what it will be. If we instead see life as a thing of potential—an infinite hallway lined with doors—endless opportunities will come our way.

You can always knock on doors in life. As deep as you go after entering a given door, you can always return to the hallway and keep experimenting with the others. Sometimes you'll enter one so good that you'll never look back; you've found your place. Other times, you'll come upon a door so inviting, so awesome, only to find that 1) when you knock, nobody answers, or 2) they do answer, but they tell you to please move on.

Ouch. We've all been there. That door seemed so wonderful! Beyond it, we thought, was everything we ever wanted. But in the end, it wasn't a door at all—it was a brick wall. This begs the question: Now what?

Even though that one door went cold, you are still surrounded by doors. When one door closes, just look around you in the hallway. The full visual landscape helps; we should imagine ourselves as surrounded by doors. This mindset helps us manifest good things, because we'll always view our lives as marked by potential, rather than stasis or limitation. If we see life as limited, we can bet that's exactly what it will be. If we instead see life as a thing of potential—an infinite hallway lined with doors—endless opportunities will come our way.

"It just wasn't meant to be" are some famous words of comfort surrounding rejection for big things in life. That's what our grandmothers tell us when things don't go our way. "There are plenty of fish in the sea" is also something we hear often, particularly regarding relationships.

As overused as they are, these kernels of wisdom are true—they're scientifically provable. The plenty-of-fish-in-the-sea one is self-explanatory. It's just like the door-lined hallway: Life is a zone of potential and opportunity. It's a place where things happen if we seek them out and allow them to unfold.

That other one, "It just wasn't meant to be," is much airier. It's a comment on fate, destiny, and the divine nature and organization of our lives' events. As such, we might be inclined—especially when still smarting from a fresh rejection—to roll our eyes at it. "Okay, Granny, thanks for rubbing salt in my wounds!" But hold on—Granny is right, and she has science to back her up.

Humans exist in linear time, which defines our waking state here on Earth. As such, when things happen, they can't un-happen. To quote Grandma once again: "You can't put the toothpaste back in the tube." What's done is done. When you look at the bigger picture, everything that has happened was, in hindsight, the only thing that could have happened. Before it happened, there were possibilities. Once it happened, though, that was it. It was in the history books.

With that in mind, everything that happens, from the beautiful to the terrible, was meant to take place. To say otherwise would be intellectually dishonest. You might wince at the "meant to" part—the whole destiny package—but as you settle into the idea that things, after they happen, could only have happened in the way they did, destiny starts seeming a lot more grounded. As life unfolds linearly, different outcomes are possible. But once the outcomes occur and the boxes beside them have been checked, that bit of the story is over. It had to go that way, in retrospect, which is why people even bother with words like destiny.

The more we get used to the way life unfolds, the more we reconcile the fact that our path becomes history as it slips into the ever-forming past. So that rejection you suffered? It *was* meant to be. It was the only way the story could have gone. Beforehand, yeah, it looked possible, but it wasn't. That tale's been told, sister.

> **Rejection hurts, and humans, as creatures of imagination, can too easily pine for what could have been. Don't pine. Move on. Knock on new doors. Life is short. There's no use in sweating what wasn't meant to be.**

Note that I'm talking to myself as much as I am to any of you. Rejection hurts, and humans, as creatures of imagination, can too easily pine for what could have been. Don't pine. Move on. Knock on new doors. Life is short. There's no use in sweating what wasn't meant to be.

Chapter Eleven
GOING WITH THE FLOW

"Feast at the banquet of knowledge and learn
all you can. There's so much we don't know."

—TILLIE VOEGTLI

When I wrote this book, I had a major blockage in my path: my awareness of my own privilege, and my fear of what I don't know. Like many of us these days, I'm conscious of intersectionality, and how social standing impacts our life outcomes. In fact, I've been on that case for a while, having been a conservative feminist for much of my life. ("Conservative feminist" and "environmentalist"—can those words exist side by side? Maybe that's my next book.)

As a woman, society imposes certain disadvantages upon me. Meanwhile, as a white person, society grants to me certain clear advantages. This has constantly been on my mind while working on this book, for the simple reason that, despite feeling that

I have much to share, I don't want to sound like a know-it-all.

After all, there's no shortage of experiences I can't understand. I can't understand a black person's experience. I can't understand a gay or bisexual or transgender person's experience. But I do know the gap between a white woman and a woman of color isn't the biggest one either woman will experience in this lifetime. And because we're all human, basic overlap exists among us. However, my ability to sympathize should not be readily mistaken for an ability to empathize.

With that in mind, as I've organized my thoughts and attempted to dispense something resembling wisdom, I've been mindful of the fact that what I'm saying—however universal it may be—will not cleanly apply to the experience of every woman or man.

That's humbling. Much as I wish I could throw my arms around the world, wrapping up my whole sisterhood in a colossal hug, at the end of the day I know my arms just don't reach that far. My experience, and the lessons I've learned from it, will never be the same as someone else's, let alone someone whose demographic profile is distinct from my own.

Here's the good news, though: There's a lesson within that humility. It involves the difference between going with and growing with the flow. The flow will be there no matter what, and we can either go with it or grow with it. Those who don't know simply go with the flow. Going has a good reputation; it's what chill people do. Just give yourself over to the current. Often, that's not a bad idea. Many times, it's our only option.

> **Much as I wish I could throw my arms around the world, wrapping up my whole sisterhood in a colossal hug, at the end of the day I know my arms just don't reach that far. My experience, and the lessons I've learned from it, will never be the same as someone else's, let alone someone whose demographic profile is distinct from my own.**

When you just go, you're not acting from a conscious place. Going doesn't take a mind—there's no calculation, strategy, mindfulness, awareness, or depth. Going, in fact, is what children do, and babies do it better than anyone—they just dance across time. It's not a bad move when you're growing up, on vacation, or simply taking a break from forcing situations to their conclusions. But as an overall life strategy, going with the flow is a terrible idea, particularly if you're interested in kicking ass and getting stuff done. If you're ambitious, if you seek to leave a mark on this world, then go ahead and try to go with the flow. Good luck! See where it gets you.

It might be a relaxing and low-pressure experience, but it'll be a shallow one because it requires zero mental rigor. The worst part is, because you're not applying your mind's resources when you go with the flow, you simply don't grow in the process because you didn't *know*.

The game is way different when you go at it consciously, with an open mind to new perspectives and people. When you're not just going, you're growing. You're working with the flow, engaging with it, studying it, learning from it. This is a whole other level of existence. You're simply not passive, but active.

The difference comes down to the extent to which you *know*. Knowing should be considered cool. Consciousness should be something to be proud of. When Trump won the 2016 presidential election, many of his opponents started calling themselves "woke," or awake to the underlying forces at work in our society, seeing through the illusion, and piercing the veil of lies. The word has an air of self-congratulation to it, but can you blame people? Look at the lies we were being asked to swallow.

When you *know*—when you're conscious, when your mind is alive—lies need not apply. You can't even pay attention to them. They come apart before you like wet tissue paper. It's something to be proud of, but it's also overwhelming. When you're not a liar, when you're not unconscious, when you're not just going with the flow, you're always learning, growing, evolving.

It makes for an intense life experience, but it's the best one to embrace if you're interested in pursuing any form of greatness or significance. I mean, look around you at the ones who excel. Does a single one of them not know? Of course not. They're chess masters. They play the game well, and their choices are backed up by their knowing. Their knowing is a product of their growing—all their failures, setbacks, rejections, disappointments, victories, breakthroughs, comebacks, and ass-kicking tours. They simply know.

Here's the paradox, though, about what you know: The more you know, the less you know. Billy Joel said it better: "The more I find out, the less that I know." That's called growing. And that's why I pointed out my privilege as a white woman. The more I come to know, the more I know about how little I know. In many ways, these privileges keep me from knowing. Like I said, I can't be someone else; I can only be me. What's the compromise, then, between me and the known limits to my knowing? Growing. Staying open. Staying receptive. Being mindful.

In the same sense, knowing involves a lot of not knowing. The more that light is shed, the more shadows are cast. The more that gets revealed, the more we become aware of what remains concealed. This is all a long-winded way of saying that knowing equals humility.

> **The game is way different when you go at it consciously, with an open mind to new perspectives and people. When you're not just going, you're growing. You're working with the flow, engaging with it, studying it, learning from it. This is a whole other level of existence.**

Like I said, to dispense knowledge or wisdom is humbling. Your humility goes hand in hand with your ongoing growth. Have you ever seen an older person who's still all clenched up with arrogance? Sheesh, Grandpa, you're ninety-two! What in the world do you still have to prove? The problem is, Grandpa doesn't know. He seeks to go, not grow.

When you grow, you'll become familiar with

humility. You'll get over yourself and gain the truest, most magnificent, and most daunting wisdom there is: for all we know, we know nothing.

Those who don't know don't even get to know that.

Chapter Twelve

THE BEST STOCK TO BET ON

"If there's one thing I'm willing
to bet on, it's myself."

—BEYONCÉ

There's the act of knowing, and then there's the entity—the person—who knows. In life, you have true, deep ownership of just this one thing. Not your home, your car, your children, your clothes, or your money. No, just *you*.

Some debate exists as to whether people continue onward beyond this life. But for the duration of life, you are the thing you can most resolutely and assertively claim ownership over.

And you are valuable. Do you know how you can confirm that? Because other people would also like to own you. Your employers seek ownership over you. Advertisers want to own you too. Anybody who's ever tried to sell you something has tried to take a piece of you. If you have children, you've experienced the extent to which they think they're the boss (note: kids have every right to this delusion, being totally dependent on you during their young lives). If you have a toxic spouse or partner, they think they're the boss of you too.

Everybody wants to own you, or co-own you, because you have something to offer, whether that's money, charm, intelligence, ability, and so on. But the unspoken deal of life is that nobody is allowed to just lay claim to you. You are your own built-in owner. Your value is yours alone.

With that in mind, you have a duty in life to cultivate yourself. Because the only thing you truly own is yourself, you have to be as awesome as possible. It's a private process—nobody else can make that happen for you.

You have a front-row seat to the show of your own life. You are an expert on yourself. Yeah, you might not know every deep, unconscious engine that's driving you, but you certainly have way more knowledge about yourself than the next person.

So ask yourself where your utmost potential lies. It's not an easy question, because experimentation is required to find out who you are. You have to dabble, trying a little bit here, a little bit there. You're not only looking out for what you like, but what others find valuable in you. Sometimes, as we've discussed, these two things won't align, and you'll have to reevaluate. If you see yourself in one role but everybody else sees you in another, only one of you has the clearer perspective. Dig deep on this stuff. Identifying your potential is the first step toward turning it into a reality.

> **You are valuable. Do you know how you can confirm that? Because other people would also like to own you. Your employers seek ownership over you. Advertisers want to own you too. Anybody who's ever tried to sell you something has tried to take a piece of you.**

As the owner of you, view yourself as a stock. You're the main—the first, perhaps the only—stock you want to invest in. This is a daily process, almost like a religion. You don't need to worship yourself, but you do need to tend to yourself.

So keep investing. With full knowledge of your potential, you'll invest wisely in yourself, practicing your trade and studying up on your interests. In the meantime, invest in your body temple—the house of you. Without it, you have nowhere to live. Don't let your most prized possession be unbalanced; your body is as important as your mind and soul.

> **When you grow with the flow, you're being daring. You're agreeing to work with, and evolve/transform through, life's wildest currents. You're not sitting this one out. You're not a sidelines player. You are out there in the water.**

It's a big responsibility, owning yourself. After all, you'll do it your whole life. Sometimes you'll get sick of or lose track of yourself. You'll think you were capable of something that you weren't. You'll think you were headed in one direction when you were really heading in another.

This is why daily mindfulness around your golden stock is essential. Like I said before, if you just go with the flow, then you're letting this beautiful lifetime pass you by. You're turning yourself into a car left in the garage under a big tarp: safe but unused, respected but certainly forgotten.

That's not what unlocking your potential looks like. In fact, the stock of you is something you must invest in repeatedly throughout your life. If you stop investing, that stock will crash. It may be a quiet crash (the car kept in the garage) or a loud one (your car flipping over off the road), but it'll be real.

At birth, you are given one thing to own and look after. You are your responsibility more than anyone else's. Invest in the one product you'll ever truly own.

It's important to mention that growing with the flow is an unsafe process. As life itself is inherently unsafe, it should come as no surprise that the growth processes we encounter within life are also unsafe. But growing with the flow isn't just any growth process; it doubles down on what's unsafe.

When you grow with the flow, you're being daring. You're agreeing to work with, and evolve/transform through, life's wildest currents. You're not sitting this one out. You're not a sidelines player. You are out there in the water.

This isn't an advisement to be reckless. Recklessness is foolish. Recklessness leaps before it looks. How can you tell the difference between recklessness, which is unhealthy, and unsafe growth, which is the best possible thing for you? It's all about the endgame, baby.

If your actions move you toward your utmost potential, honoring what you have to offer this world, then by definition they can't be reckless; they can only be bold. The intention and the outcome are partners in crime. What you seek defines the nature of how you seek it.

If your actions move you toward something ill-defined, for the sake of claiming excitement or testing the waters, they won't necessarily kill you, but they'll still be reckless. That's why young people are more experimental: they haven't yet learned to put a cork in their recklessness. But if you're reckless in enough situations, you do learn to cool it eventually.

Let's bring back our handy stock metaphor: Investing in yourself cannot be reckless. In fact, it's the wisest, most self-loving thing you can do. When you love yourself, you stand a darn good chance at loving the world, which will only enhance your value in it.

Recklessness occurs when you invest elsewhere. When you lose the trail, when the goal gets murky, when you're out for kicks—that's when the outcomes will suddenly cease to serve you. Then you'll be upside down in a ditch, asking, "How did I get here?"

Move unsafely, but don't be reckless. Embrace the wildness. Befriend unpredictability. Explode your own potential. Once you open up one box of potential, believe me, there'll be another box waiting there within it, then another box inside that one . . .

Keep tearing those boxes open. In time, you'll learn what all who risk investing in themselves come to know: your stock can never, ever stop growing, for your potential is truly limitless.

Chapter Thirteen

LEARNING TO RECEIVE

"You have to find a tribe."

—RuPaul

In March of 2018, the year after Hurricane Harvey, we finally moved back home. It wasn't the same home as the previous one, of course. We found ourselves in a brand-new house, one we were lucky to occupy. It always takes time to settle after moving, often more time than we admit we need. There's the physical transition, followed by the mental one, then the emotional one.

A planned, intended move is one thing. A move that's been forced upon you by a hurricane is another thing entirely. This is not to say I didn't feel grateful. In fact, looking around at our new surroundings, I knew our being there was intensely tied to the fact that we'd had a supportive village around us. There's no other reasonable interpretation of how our relocation came to be—other people held us up, supported us, and literally carried us home.

Receiving help of any kind has always been a nightmare for me. Allowing the aid of our village called me to receive on a more profound level than I ever had before. Among the many lessons bestowed upon me by Harvey, this one was by far the most striking and meaningful: receive.

I couldn't believe I was in a position to. Forgive me if that sounds snobby. It's not that I deemed myself immune to being down; quite the contrary, I've spent a great deal of my life on the floor (figuratively and literally, as we'll soon see), gasping for air, straining to get back up. But I'd always somehow managed to sidestep receiving. Every time I successfully kept my door shut and didn't let another person's generosity in, I felt as though I had accomplished something.

The reason for this links back to how Dad always told me to be independent. He always drilled it into me that we weren't the type of people who held our hands out. That alone was a powerful starting point for my attitude about receiving, but I could also blame it on astrology. I'm a Capricorn, for heaven's sake; a goat—the most stubborn sign in the lot. A goat is not out looking for support. It just trudges ahead, being tough and getting the job done. Little do people know, however, that beneath their rugged exteriors, goats are sensitive and vulnerable creatures, just like everybody else—but we go to incredible lengths to avoid showing it.

When you really strip back all the layers, I'm sure my general inability to receive stemmed from a basic sense of low self-worth. On the surface, that seems crazy. After all, I'm ambitious, driven, confident, outspoken, and optimistic. I have high hopes, and I go after what I want. I work to inspire. I try to *be* inspired. That's hardly the description of someone with self-worth issues.

Receiving help of any kind has always been a nightmare for me. Allowing the aid of our village called me to receive on a more profound level than I ever had before. Among the many lessons bestowed upon me by Harvey, this one was by far the most striking and meaningful: receive.

The thing is, those traits represent somebody who is actively pushing back against her own insufficient sense of self-worth. Your ambitious side pushes back against failure; your drive pushes back against your laziness; your confidence wages a war against your low self-esteem. This is a dance we carry out with ourselves, and it casts strong illusions in all directions. It makes the successful among us look strong, when the truth is they're often simply revolting against their own weaknesses.

What do we do, then, in the midst of this duality ping-pong game? If we're driven to achieve and succeed, it seems like the endgame is to triumph over our weak parts. The real trick, however, is to dance with the weak side—the side that's dark, slovenly, unkempt, embarrassing, and vulnerable. It's about knowing when to let the shadow come out to play. This is a sexy way of saying it's about knowing when to just let go and admit that, yes, we're a freaking hot mess.

For some people, this comes naturally—but I'm not necessarily commending them. Some people's problems are the opposite of mine: they're out for too much support. Their hands are constantly outstretched because they think they can't do it on their own. They need nonstop help and positive reinforcement. Do you hear the criticism in my words? Are you seeing how against this attitude I've been conditioned to be? For these people, the trick is to dance with their strength. They have to allow themselves to be the ones in charge. They have to let go of the side of the pool and learn to swim, absent any support.

Most of us, I'm sure, are somewhere between the two extremes. We have our strong points and our weak points. Under some circumstances, we thrive; under others, we quiver.

Not me, though (goats aren't very graceful dancers). I wasn't in between; I was out to prove how strong and independent I was. I didn't even realize it consciously. I'd hypnotized myself into thinking I could be 100 percent independent, 100 percent of the time.

And it worked! Until it didn't. Then it all came crashing down.

Flashback to Hurricane Harvey. There we were in the storm. Cue the special effects—the lightning, rain, wind, and thunder beating down our house. Going back to these memories is like stepping onto a ride at Disney Land . . . only less fun.

It was boat time. We had no other options. Already, it seemed clear that our material possessions were fast becoming things of the past, so far be it from me to let my two most prized possessions—Mark and Ally—slip through my fingers. I had no choice but to make the call, but Mark didn't want to. In his mind, things had not yet become that extreme. But one look at the water coursing past our front door, and it didn't exactly seem like we were headed out on a walk. Maybe Mark could have handled it. I certainly wasn't as reliable. As for Ally? Forget it; she was too small, too scared, too vulnerable—not unlike me.

All through the night, I had been doing my damnedest to be of use to others. Through social media, I'd been facilitating the flow of information and communication. I had perceived myself as a helper, so that was the job I readily undertook. Now, though, the flow (all puns intended) had reversed.

You know the basic airline safety instruction to put on your own oxygen mask before helping the person beside you? That's always struck me as wise and grounded advice, for use in everyday life. Why do airlines even have to say that? It should be common knowledge that we're of no use to others if we're not ourselves receiving help. Apparently not—as evidenced by the fact that the airlines need to say it, our human inclination is to jump in and start being helpful while neglecting our own selves.

My time had come, though. I'd done it wrong all night long, throwing my energy toward others but paying scant attention to my own needs. Now, in belated fashion, it was time for me to put on my own mask first.

I cannot overstate what an overpowering moment of surrender this was. With hindsight, I'm able to put it into more meaningful context of my own growth and evolution. In the moment, though, it looked different. I wasn't even fully present. I was more animal than human, fighting against a real apocalypse, or at least a perfect simulation of one.

When the man with the boat showed up at our door, neither Mark nor myself knew how to behave. We were both getting F-minuses in the receiving department, forgetting that sometimes other people like to give too, for nothing else than giving's own sake.

Riding on that boat, I felt like a stranger in my own life. Not only were my home, husband, and dog receding into the background, but I had given myself over to a complete stranger. This had nothing to do with trust. In fact, I trusted that man entirely. He was a good Samaritan who wanted to save us. No, I felt strange because I was the passenger rather than the driver.

Which, in a way, all of us are. It all comes down to growing with the flow. As the flow carried us out of our neighborhood, little did I know I was growing with it. Looking back, I see how that terrifying yet beautiful moment in time was a stunning symbol for life in general: we're not the drivers; we are the passengers. This isn't meant to encourage a passive mentality but to throw a big shout-out to the concept of surrender.

"We make plans. God laughs." I don't really throw down with this saying. If there is a God, I don't think she's cruel. I do, however, think that when we make plans, God looks on with impassive neutrality, for God has plenty of plans of her own.

Imagine if I had not surrendered. Imagine if I'd let my own illusion of control, of being in charge, of being the giver and not the receiver, predominate in that situation. I wouldn't have been much of a controller or giver in the end, would I? No, because I would have been dead.

When you don't have formal insurance, you better hope you carry informal insurance. Informal insurance comes in one form only: other people, my tribe. Only when others came to my side did I learn how to receive. The Sheryl Sandberg and Dave Goldberg Family Foundation; my father; my mother; my sister, Aimee, and in-laws, Brian, Frank, and Karen; my bestie, Jennifer Emerson; my maid of honor, Ame Cameron—among too many others to name and count (although I did my best in the acknowledgments)—came swinging to my family's rescue.

Ironically, in the course of my work, I've often told women, "Lean in! Step up to the table!" Funny how we confuse ourselves into seeing the lean as ours alone, and the table as anything but round. If you're going to encourage people to lean in, you better not reject their help when they come to offer it. Not only is accepting help good manners, but it's also critical to our survival. Empowerment needn't be a top-down process, wherein the queen bee empowers all the worker bees, then the worker bees go off to live productive lives. No, the queen needs tons of help as well—to the point where it's a joke to think of her as a queen.

The world economy is changing. We've only known it to be top-down, vertical, above and below, but now it's tilting horizontally. We're seeing innumerable forms of equality emerge, and the ascent of women is just one of them. For the longest time, boardroom tables have been rectangular. I'm foreseeing a future in which they're round, everybody equal, all eyes accessible, all voices speaking from the exact same distance.

That's how things have always been, anyway. You know that old saying "Behind every successful man is a successful woman"—why not replace "behind" with "beside"? If my success is my husband's success, and his success is mine, then even though we have each other's backs, neither one of us is remotely behind the other. That's just bad form, literally. We stand united. So it should go for women and society in total.

Great companies might be launched by singular visionaries, but they require great teams to keep them going. Everybody knows this, yet the accolades are still funneled to the top. This illusion is rapidly breaking down. We're seeing that the top is down here, the table is round, and the layout is horizontal. The queen bee is just a worker, and the workers are queens. It cannot be any other way.

Everything I know about networking—at least, all the good stuff about it—I can trace back to Lori Feldman, the aforementioned powerhouse business executive in St. Louis who owns her own marketing company. I met Lori back in the days before LinkedIn, before networks were automated and readymade for you to opt into. Back then, we had to build them on our own from scratch.

Not long ago, my husband was going through his shoebox of old business cards. It was good for a laugh—the laminated cards got the most points. Oh, the trouble people used to go through in pursuit of impressive business cards. People still trade cards, of course, but we know it makes more sense to let a tree live and just punch the person's number into your phone. (I figure it'll be ten more years until we have chips in our brains that permanently store the numbers, but let's not get ahead of ourselves.)

Lori didn't teach me how to lay down a network piece by piece, like a railroad track. Instead, she and my mother both shared with me something far more nuanced: the value of putting deposits down on your future and building a tribe by being a lifelong giver and connector. Adam Grant, author of *Give and Take: A Revolutionary Approach to Success*, says, "Being a giver is not good for the 100-yard dash, but it's valuable in the marathon."

> **The world economy is changing. We've only known it to be top-down, vertical, above and below, but now it's tilting horizontally. We're seeing innumerable forms of equality emerge, and the ascent of women is just one of them.**

For starters, being a giver is the right thing to do. Doing right by people (and the environment, for that matter) creates the invaluable preconditions for people to do right by you. Will all of them come back to you, boomerang-style, and do so? Not at all. But when you build a community of givers and receivers, you have to remember that you can and should play both roles. Grant also says, "If we create networks with the sole intention of getting something, we won't succeed. We can't pursue the benefit of networks; the benefits ensue from investments in meaningful activities and relationships." Grant is spot on.

The good news is that a delightfully surprising number of those you've helped will absolutely help you someday. I followed Lori's advice about paying it forward without ever expecting the boomerang to fly back my way. It felt like good sense, like having a bank account.

And I never had to withdraw any money. That moment when I put out the word that I needed the boat during Hurricane Harvey was an exception. I made the call and asked for help. I fell backward into the arms of the universe, in a state of glorious surrender. Asking my network for help was a withdrawal.

Oddly, most of the deposits I've made on my future have come back without me asking for them at all.

Asking and receiving are two different things, and sometimes they go together. Often, they don't. Both require exertion, to varying degrees. When you're asking, you're putting yourself out there. You're holding your hands out, saying, "Hey, um, over here! I need help!" Sometimes that leads to receiving.

When you receive, you're exerting in a whole other way. It's the exertion of surrender, like taking a yoga class and focusing on going loose: loose muscles, loose mind, loose soul. As anybody who's done yoga can tell you, that takes effort. Oftentimes, we're all clenched up. And receiving when you haven't even asked? Whoa, that's a whole other level.

I'd built a network that wasn't just professional or familial; it had different gradients. A great deal of it had been woven online: Facebook, WhatsApp, Twitter, Instagram, even LinkedIn. While the storm was raging, my whole network lit up. Its local branches were in constant communication. I felt like a dispatcher camped out before a microphone, coordinating, connecting, checking, rechecking, looking into, reconfirming, and doubling back.

In hindsight, putting aside whatever self-worth issues I might be grappling with, it makes sense that my network swooped in to help me. Even though that outcome had never been my intention, that's simply how networks work: horizontally. Everybody is wired to everybody else. Nobody is up in some distant fortress, hovering away from the common people. In fact, isolation is a pretty dangerous tactic. Much as we may fantasize about becoming hugely wealthy and disappearing into a secret cavern three hundred miles below the earth, we need people to thrive. We have to stay connected and keep our networks running.

Mine was running so hot after the storm that I couldn't keep up with it. After I put out the call for the boat, I didn't have to ask for much of anything. It was already flowing in my direction before I had to say anything. Getting a front-row seat to the goodness of other humans was the strangest aspect of the storm's aftermath. I saw love in action rather than expressed through sentiment. Some people call themselves humbled after seeing such things, but if I'm to be honest, no word can truly capture how it made me feel. I was stunned silent, on my knees with gratitude.

Relationships, I saw, are bridges, and good bridges run in both directions. As Deepak Chopra can tell you, giving and receiving are two sides of a coin. They're both expressions of the same energy, running in two different directions. Knowing this, you can see how if you don't understand one, you really don't understand the other. I'd deemed myself an expert on giving, but I was a total amateur in the receiving department at the time because I didn't truly understand giving to its fullest.

It's one thing to give with no expectation of anything in return. That's as it should be, and that's what I'd long seen myself doing. Upon closer look, however, it wasn't that I didn't expect anything in return, but that I didn't *want* anything in return. Not expecting isn't the same as not wanting. This is the difference between someone who's chill and casual and someone who's locked in an airtight state of control. When you don't expect something, you can accept the outcome no matter which way it goes. When you don't want something, you're keeping a wall up in preemptive self-defeat—and walls are the opposite of bridges.

As the expression goes, the givers gain. This does not mean giving should be motivated by gaining, because most of the time you actually won't gain—at least not in the near-term, nor from the exact people you initially gave to.

Beyond that, know that giving, in addition to being the right thing to do, is actually pleasure-producing. There's a release involved. It's like when you go to your grandma's house for dinner and she sends you home with piles of leftovers. She loves doing it; she wants you fed and happy. But she also has a deep *need* to do it—she can't help herself. It's that power of release, letting go, not hoarding your goods, spreading the wealth, or communicating to others that what's mine is yours.

And you know what makes Grandma go berserk? When you say, "What's mine is yours too." No, no, no, no. She won't have it. Talk about throwing up walls and burning bridges! No way is Grandma going to take a single thing from you, her precious grandchild.

We'll give her a pass because she's Grandma. It's too late to talk any sense into her. But you and me?

We aren't getting a pass. Our bridges must be open for business—two lanes, both directions, no exceptions, open all day, and accessible at night.

I know it's hard. We're conditioned to be caretakers, hardwired to be constantly proving ourselves. The things we take feel like burdens, like they're ten thousand times the magnitude of everything we ever gave. And it's like, "Great. How do we ever balance out this scale?"

We don't, because it's not a scale. The endgame isn't balance, but abundance. Give, give, give. You're planting seeds. You don't know which ones will end up sprouting flowers, but that's not important. You're feeding Mother Earth. Sometimes she'll grant you flowers; sometimes she'll grant you nothing tangible. Much of the time, all you'll get back is the quiet comfort of knowing that you gave—which is a lot.

Sometimes, though—oh, man—beautiful flowers end up growing. Mother Earth will throw you a giant party. She generally won't do it for no reason whatsoever. Nah, she's not into trivial gestures. She'll wait until you're the one in need, down on your knees in prayer, doubtful, desperate, and waiting for a miracle. Then she'll come. But only if you planted seeds.

When those flowers grow and you witness all their glory, you'll realize that although the miracle was one of nature, it also had another, special, sacred source: you.

The giver gains the goodwill of others; that much is clear. But the giver gains well beyond that. The giver also gains power. It's not the kind of power we're accustomed to, where someone has leverage or advantages over others. The problem with that worldview is that it's based in scarcity. It suggests that in order for some to have, others must go without. We've witnessed this pattern throughout history. Some are up, others down. But like I said, the field has been quickly tilting from vertical to horizontal, the table shifting from rectangular to round. I'm not saying the whole game is bound to change overnight, but true equality doesn't have to remain some far-off fantasy. Its outlines are coming into crisp, clear focus. And when it comes, believe me, it won't be defined by scarcity.

Power doesn't have to be about leverage or advantage; it can be about access, openness, and sharing. In fact, I'd argue the latter form of power is way more . . . powerful. Givers gain respect and loyalty—essentially, a posse. We don't always know who's in the posse, as Hurricane Harvey taught me. Some whom I assumed were in it weren't, and others whose relationship to me had been unknown most certainly were. As you give, little by little, you build your posse.

That posse is your power (among all your other good traits, gifts, and wisdom). Power isn't having people below you, answering to you while secretly hoping for your downfall. That position affords us the illusion of power, but the clock is always ticking on that illusion. In time, it's bound to run out.

More sustainable power exists in network fashion, where the field is already horizontal and the table is round. Every time you give, you're demonstrating respect. Most times, when you respect other people, you gain respect in return. If you don't, no biggie; you've learned who not to give to anymore. In general, however, just keep giving, over and over. Keep building the network. Keep building your power.

I'm a strong proponent of building networks because, early in life, I realized I have a knack for connecting. I'm never one to hesitate to chat up a stranger. In fact, it's kind of like a superpower. But like all superpowers, this one has its downsides. I can make the connections, I can build the networks, I can get cool people in my corner—but I can be too trusting.

Funny how what propels us can almost always seriously hinder us. It's like this human system was designed that way—there always has to be a catch, a paradox, a limit to our power, applied by that very power itself. This is where your confidantes are important.

This doesn't apply only to building networks and/or being trustworthy. No matter who you are, what your powers are, and what your accordant limitations are, you need confidantes in your corner—real ones, not passive, overeager yes-women—to get authentic feedback and bounce things off of.

As much as my husband drives me up the wall (as I do him), he's still my rock, in my corner, on my side, and absolutely ready to fight for me. In fact, Mark's natural mindset is a perfect complement to my own. Whereas I'm Ms. Chatty and can thus be too open and trusting, Mark casts a more skeptical eye on people. Maybe this is a classic masculine-feminine dichotomy. Whatever the root, it's good to have him there. I'll be welcoming some soul with open arms, and Mark will be like, "Hold on, wait a second . . ." I'm grateful to have my positivity bias, and accordingly I can become irritated when Mark displays his counter-bias—but often, that dude has a point.

The givers gain. In contrast, we have takers. Takers—it should come as no surprise—always lose. Or maybe it is a surprise to the takers! After all, they're always on the take, so it must sneak up on them when they find that, in the end, they have two fistfuls of sand.

Takers lose because they bunch up the flow of energy. They're dead ends, energy-wise, and it's always a bummer when you hit one. It breaks the flow you had when you were driving, bunching up all that energy you'd been gliding along on. You have to regroup, turn around, and get your bearings again.

Takers, on some psychological level, are convinced that life has been less than fair to them. They perceive that others are always getting more, so they don't feel guilty about taking. Sticking their hand in the pot too many times seems fair, and they have a major blind spot when it comes to perceiving the worth other people put in. This blind spot is the taker's most prominent symptom. Whatever they're interested in taking, they're most blind to seeing others deserving. If they're interested in taking your time, they simply believe they alone are starved for time and thus deserve to take a lot of it, whereas you probably have your whole situation under control and can thus stand to spare a little time.

Money is a more vivid example. If you have any, somebody will want some (if not all) of it. Many people are perfectly willing to work for it, or to gain it through a fair and equitable arrangement. Others have a bank-robber mentality, like, "Look, she already has lots of money. Our little theft won't hurt her." Even though takers lose over the long-term (they're always locked in such a scarcity mentality that they take continuously), they most certainly gain over the short-term. And they do so at your expense.

Are some people straddled on the fence, givers sometimes and takers others? I don't think so. Sure, people can be needier in some departments than in

> **Power doesn't have to be about leverage or advantage; it can be about access, openness, and sharing. In fact, I'd argue the latter form of power is way more . . . powerful.**

others. But in general, your inclinations lean one way or the other. If you give and give, yet tax it and take back something massive in return (without any prior arrangement or agreement), then you weren't giving at all.

It all goes back to how giving and receiving are one thing. To understand one is to understand the other. With that in mind, it's unlikely that you'll look at a person and be like, "Oh, Sheila? Yeah, she's generous a lot of the time, but she's also selfish too." Nonsense. Whatever your failings and limitations, if you're a giver, you're a giver—because you understand giving from the inside out. You know its power, its value, and its contribution to the overriding flow.

Likewise, if you're a taker, that's the gear you're driving in. You can always switch gears and do better, but don't delude yourself into thinking you're a-okay half the time, because whatever you're taking more than offsets what you're giving.

My mother has always been a Major League Giver. She feels honor-bound, obligated. She's not a martyr, though; that's just the way she rolls. I got this from her. In my mind, I see the power of it. But I realize that every time I whip out my coin purse, some people see me as a flashing neon sign that reads "Open for Business."

It's a shame. It's particularly sad because those who don't have the taking mentality have trouble recognizing or relating to those who do. We thus get sneaked up on all the time. We can't believe people would actually be so cruel. Learning to recognize takers requires practice.

Chapter Fourteen

TRAVEL LIGHTLY

"If you are working on something exciting
that you really care about, you don't have
to be pushed. The vision pulls you."

—STEVE JOBS

I'll never forget the night before my house took on water. It's seared in memory, still fresh as of this writing, but it somehow feels ancient on account of its unquestionable permanence.

When you're getting ready to flee, you think to pack. Naturally, the night before Harvey arrived, I put a bag together. But two things I truly needed, more than anything else, I had to cling to the tightest: my husband and my daughter. Okay, and our dog, Maddie, too!

The bag had some handy incidentals. My family, however, wasn't incidental. They were, and remain, essential. So I held them close, and we cried.

I wrote in chapter 12 about how you are your most valuable property, and thus the stock most worth investing in. But a key investment within is the part of yourself that stands to grant you the greatest possible life—the part of yourself that has the ability to love.

> **As you grow with the flow, you do not grow alone. Yes, on a fundamental level, all of us are traveling solo through this world, but around us are layers of companionship and human fortification. Our colleagues, teammates, mentors, and cheer squad are precious, but something of an outer layer.**

There's you, of course, but there's also other people. Most of them you will not necessarily love. You might love all of humanity with your giant heart, but only a treasured few will stand to gain the intimate radiance of your deepest and most sincere love. These are the ones who will make your life worth living.

As you grow with the flow, you do not grow alone. Yes, on a fundamental level, all of us are traveling solo through this world, but around us are layers of companionship and human fortification. Our colleagues, teammates, mentors, and cheer squad are precious, but something of an outer layer. Our intimate loved ones are the innermost layer imaginable; they're the ones who share your life with you. They're the ones who, like it or not, give you feedback. They're the ones you call first when there's a problem. Their presence—and their ability to support, guide, and/or correct you—is not only a sweet thing to behold, but a major catalyst for your ability to grow.

My family's record books have never known a crisis or a horror worse than Hurricane Harvey. It was devastating. Its echoes still ring in my ears. But—forgive the cliché—it was all the more manageable because we went through it together. Yeah, we got on each other's nerves. In the heat of the moment, everything seemed so upside down. But as I reflect, I feel grateful not only for having lived through it, but for having seen my beautiful family live through it too.

Without question, the hardest parts of growing with the flow are the times of calamity. The times when transformation is thrust upon you. The days when the fates and the universe conspire to say, "You know what? That familiar version of yourself that you've relied on up until now, the one that got you this far? We're going to shatter it and cue up a new one."

Sure, it may sound poetic, but living through it is a whole other story. When you grow with the flow, you don't get to decide how intense the waves and currents are. That's out of your hands. In your hands is your reaction and, if you're lucky, the ones you hold dear.

In the movies, times of calamity come and go with speed. A crisis erupts in Act 1, but the skies are clear again a couple hours later, come Act 3. In real life, it's a much slower, more grueling process. You wake up in the morning with a moment of light and gentle simplicity, then say to yourself, "Oh, I'm still in the middle of this nightmare." Sometimes it even happens in the middle of the night. You get up to use the bathroom. You're just a body, absent a mind, until your brain says, "Wait, isn't something supposed to be wrong right now?" Then you remember that thing you are going through.

Remember, this too shall pass. When it does, your most amazing and moving memories of it will be those of your encounters and discussions with your loved ones as the whole dang episode unfolded. And you will swell with gratitude that they were there.

Here's the thing, though: You have to travel lightly. Do not stuff too much into your bag (the real one or the figurative one). When the flow gets harsh, you don't want to be bogged down with too many heavy things: details, obligations, unsolved problems, unruly activity, static noise. No, keep it simple and pack a light bag—just you, yourself, and the ones you love.

If you find yourself loving nobody right now, trust me that you're not alone in your solitude. Loving ain't easy. The ones we love the most drive us the craziest—that's the price we pay for agreeing to intermingle our world with theirs. But in the end, your company, their nourishing support, and your new shared narrative are beyond worth it, should we be so lucky to have these things. The trick to accessing them is traveling light. This is another way of saying: Get your priorities straight.

> **When you grow with the flow, you don't get to decide how intense the waves and currents are. That's out of your hands. In your hands is your reaction and, if you're lucky, the ones you hold dear.**

A woman with too many priorities is a woman with too many problems. When you travel light, you keep your problem count low. Then, when a real storm comes, you're ready for it. And the flow won't overwhelm you as it takes you.

Chapter Fifteen

E3, P3

"Energy, equality, and economy . . .
through people, passion, and purpose."

—KATIE MEHNERT

I wrote down the above words on my fabled airplane cocktail napkin. I thought "E3, P3" sounded catchy— not a strength one should underestimate when communicating one's ideas. Moreover, the very substance of the construct carried major water.

Energy is the field I'm in, and it's what the whole world runs on. I'm not just talking about the energy that keeps our homes heated and our cars in motion; I'm also talking about fundamental energy: the stuff that makes our eyes blink and our lungs expand. This plane we live on is made of energy. My career has dealt with the industrial kind, which is just a formalized offshoot of the fundamental energy at the very center of our earthly existence. To provide quality energy, you have to understand that it's not just a product; it's a life source. It's not only about industrial machinery, but spiritual machinery too.

> **Men brought industry to the world. In doing so, they created and provided profound, amazing value. But things have changed, and our growth has bent around to bite us in our backsides. We lack sustainability in terms of energy, and we cannot reach sustainability without equality.**

Equality is just as important. Energy might be monolithic and apply to everyone and everything, but we know there is no peace between everyone and everything without equality. America's discussion around equality has reached a fever pitch in recent days. Those on the left demand equality for women, minorities, and other marginalized groups. Those on the right insist that the less government and the more freedom we have, the more equality will happen on its own.

I think most of us, no matter where we land on the spectrum, are becoming exhausted from this chatter.

We're in an age in which politics hinder more than they help, or are not nearly as efficient as we prefer. Everyone loses out as a result, but one lady loses out most of all: Mother Earth.

Are you bugging out over this connection yet? Yes, energy and equality are basically inseparable. Mother Earth, which we've deemed feminine, has been pushed to the side. I'm not just being metaphorical; it's no accident that nature has taken a back seat to what humans consider progress. And it's no accident that our natural environment is constantly stomped on by the feet of men.

I'm talking about the systems of men since time immemorial. Men brought industry to the world. In doing so, they created and provided profound, amazing value. But things have changed, and our growth has bent around to bite us in our backsides. We lack sustainability in terms of energy, and we cannot reach sustainability without equality.

Mother Earth must be relieved of her marginalized status (and fast, because she's been *pissed* lately). And literal mothers, women, people of color, LGBTQ+ people, disabled people, and those who are downtrodden, left out, or kicked aside—all of us must be granted relief as well.

Mind you, men should not be excluded from this journey; we need them along for the ride. This is not about some of us rising up so that others can be brought down. This is about all of us rising up as one, and *now*.

Everybody can be part of the energy narrative. Everybody can pitch in to get us out of the last century and into the current one. And everybody can line up with pride, without being robbed of self-worth or basic resources, so that we can finally have Mother Earth's back.

Economy is a natural principle here too. If you take care of energy in a spirit of equality, then the economy becomes unstoppable. Right now, we have an economy in which those at the top win and those at the (immensely expanding) bottom keep on losing. It's been termed by some as a zombie economy—a pale, ambling substitute for the real thing.

The real thing is inclusive. The real thing has many more seats at the table. The real thing isn't built on fear, nor an absurd sense of scarcity that sends us scrambling for our piece of the pie and diminishing those whom we think would steal pie from our plates. The real thing gets me up every day; my vision of it pulls me.

There's plenty of pie to go around. In fact, the opportunity to reinvent our world's energy systems is an all-hands-on-deck affair. We need everybody aboard this ride—female, male, privileged, disadvantaged. You are needed. We face this future together.

People. Like it or not, life is all about them. Our

differences, while often aggravating, accumulate into our shared strengths. The human race thrives on its diversity of not only backgrounds, but mindsets and skill sets. So bring on *all* the people! Energy isn't often considered a social field, but it is. It's about connections, community, collaboration, and cross-pollination.

> **Everybody can be part of the energy narrative. Everybody can pitch in to get us out of the last century and into the current one. And everybody can line up with pride, without being robbed of self-worth or basic resources, so that we can finally have Mother Earth's back.**

Passion. How are we going to climb this mountain, to transition from the old energy format to the bright, green new one? You can't make this climb with a sigh and a yawn. No, you need an energy all its own to do so, and that energy is ideally pure human passion. People without passion are a pitiful sight, but people with passion are un-freaking-stoppable.

Purpose. We've pretty much nailed this one to

the floor. Not everyone has to be an engineer, but everyone has to be aboard for the future. The purpose, therefore, is for us to survive. And let's take it a step further and *thrive*. Survival can too easily become passionless—only passion, from wherever one pulls it, will allow one to actually thrive.

> **How are we going to climb this mountain, to transition from the old energy format to the bright, green new one? You need an energy all its own to do so, and that energy is ideally pure human passion. People with passion are un-freaking-stoppable.**

E3, P3. Plain and simple. When I came up with this concept, I'd grown tired of energy getting a bad rap. I realized that if we didn't own this story, and if I didn't do my best to strip politics out of the equation and get a serious conversation going around equality, economy, and energy, then nothing had a chance at changing.

Sure, when I defined these principles on that airplane napkin, I was a raging madwoman. I was drunk on wine, half out of my gourd. But I also knew of some other bold madpeople, whose historical examples had set the precedent for my own work in the twenty-first century: the original wildcatters who'd brought the oil industry into being. We're talking about entrepreneurs back in the pre-digital age, when energy ran on steam and coal. Crazy as they were, they're a big part of the reason—and perhaps the main reason—why life is so comfortable today compared to then. Their work spurred monumental technological advances. It lifted nations out of poverty. Yet (here it comes) it had one aspect that would someday, long after they were all gone, come back to haunt them: all this work was done by men.

This isn't reverse sexism. I just said a few pages ago that I want men at the table because all ships, remember, rise with the tide. But we've hit a breaking point. The onslaught of masculine energy that's brought us to where we are now needs to be tempered. Note that I said "masculine energy," not "men." Masculine energy is aggressive and assertive. It wants to push, propel, compel, confront, leap, kick, and jab. Masculine energy is immensely beautiful. Heck, it's half the circle of life. You're not going to catch me hating on it. It is, I say again, the reason why life has been so comfortable in this century.

Yet feminine energy offers an—I use this word intently—alternative. Feminine energy is about balance, nurturing, compassion, creativity, and love.

Again, I didn't say "women." Countless men have those traits as well, and countless women don't. But what's needed to pull the oil industry into this current century where it belongs, so as to allow it not just to survive, but to thrive, is a major infusion of feminine energy.

And here I am. But I can't do this alone, of course. I aim to harness as much feminine energy as I can, from myself, from other women, from men, from Mother Earth. Together, we need to compassionately and consciously tip the conversation around energy into a direction that enables human survival.

It can be done. If you call me a madwoman, that's okay. I've already called myself that, and I've already touched upon the madness of my predecessors. But riddle me this: Where are the madmen presently leading the charge when it comes to our energy problem?

They're nowhere. They don't exist. Many years ago, then-CEO of BP, John Browne, pushed the industry to think about the future and embrace renewables. Browne was met with intense criticism. He was a visionary ahead of his time, yet a powerful messenger. From him and others, we need to take the torch. And by "we," I mean those willing to utilize the feminine to transition our world onto a more sustainable path.

Wall Street is all about bulls and bears. Washington is a game played by elephants and donkeys. Silicon Valley is a monument built by nerds in garages drinking Pepsi. Across the ages, we've seen masculine energy in varying forms assert itself across all society's major pillars.

The tide is shifting now, and *everyone* must hang on and grow with the flow.

ACKNOWLEDGMENTS

It's taken me way too long to publish this book. I started writing it nearly twenty years ago. Putting yourself out there isn't easy, but the world needs people who will move it forward. We need dreamers, believers, influencers, changemakers, and rainmakers. We need people who want to grow themselves and their communities to be more equal, connected, resilient, and sustainable.

When we are born, we enter the world cold and naked, amidst blood, sweat, and tears. While it sounds morbid, we are all born and then on to our journey to death. What matters is the space in between: the days, nights, weeks, months, and years that shape us into who we become. It's those stories we need to share, with the hopes of creating a community of learning and, above all, growth.

We have a choice in life: we can go with the flow or grow with it. Growth is taking all that life gives us and moving forward. It's about progression. It's about taking the good and the bad and making meaning and purpose. It's about building a tremendous amount of grit and flexing that muscle when we need to make another leap and grow. Triumphs, setbacks, happiness, and sorrow are all part of this journey. Our experiences and the human connections we create matter most in the journey.

I want to thank my peeps, my tribe, for without them this book and these memories would not be possible.

I thank my family. I cannot image life without Mark, Ally, and our grandoodle, Maddie Mehnert. Mark is my rock and the reason I am able to do so much. He's a great father with a sense of humor that keeps me laughing and loving him and our life each and every day, despite how messy it gets. My daughter, Ally, is my true north. She is with me wherever I "grow." I get up every day because I want a better world for her. I thank my parents, Kay and Lance Walthall. Both are fiercely independent and helped me grow in many ways and have given me so many tools in my success. I thank my sisters, Aimee and Sarah, whom I fought with and will forever love. I also thank my extended family, including my stepmother, Bradley, and my in-laws, Karen and Frank Skowronski. I also thank Barbara Blevins, Lynda Carson, Carmen Moore, Myra Porter, and Katia Trancoso, who have taken special interest in Ally and helped me tremendously in my journey as a parent.

I thank my friends. It took me seventeen years to find a bestie, Jennifer Martinez Emerson, whom I met through a women's resource group at Shell. Jeni has been there for me in my happiest and darkest moments. We have grown so much in this time and have been blessed to raise resilient children in what sometimes feels like an unsustainable world.

I also thank Lori Feldman, a tremendous mentor and friend; my sorority sisters, Kerri Driscoll and Jen Schneider; my maid of honor, Ame Cameron; and my fast running buddy, Janet Ware, who are always a phone call away when I need a good laugh, cry, or swift kick in the ass. And to the mommies who've made motherhood while working fun, I give my thanks: Stacey Cline, Laura Faulkenberry, Blair Heiligbrodt, Melissa Herring, Lindsay Massengill, Victoria Meyer, Michelle Priest, Joy Austin Ramsaran, Zulfia Samedova, Melissa Simpson, Alyssa Snider, Tonya Spell, Andrea Stevens, Martha St. John, Laura Whiles, Chrissie Welch, Erin Verdon, and Candida Wolfram.

I thank my teachers, those who taught me and helped me grow in so many ways. The late Hannah Rucker, my high school English teacher, who hand-picked me to be part of her leadership class. Hannah had stage-four breast cancer and drove to Houston to celebrate my wedding in 2009. She fought cancer valiantly and lost that battle in 2016. There isn't a day that goes by that I don't think of her laugh, and I know she'd be proud I finally published this book. I also thank Tillie Voegtli, my college marketing professor, who gave me a place to shine once I found my voice. To Sister Teresita Rivet at Ursuline Academy, one tough nun who reared me in the early days and taught me the early tenets of diversity and inclusion. **I thank my angels.** These leaders have been instrumental to helping me grow professionally and personally. I thank Peggy Montana, former chairman and CEO of Shell Midstream, and a selfless engineer who gave me a path in energy so could I go on to do bigger things. I'm grateful for her sponsorship over the years and all she's done to help me become a CEO. I also thank Cindy Patman for giving me seed investment for Pink Petro (over a nice glass of wine), and former CEO of Jive Software Elisa Steele, who gave me the tech platform to build our proof of concept. I also thank Melody Meyer for sharing a common passion for the role of women in our energy transition and her ongoing wisdom support. I also thank Lynda Attaway, Carol Battershell, Kathleen Camilli, Elizabeth (Libby) Cheney, Donna Cole, Christy Dillard, Susan Hodge, Carissa Janeway, June Ressler, and Hilary Ware for countless calls and coaching. To the men who shaped my work and life, I thank John Sequiera for his D&I wisdom, and Sean Guerre and Jason Korman for their mentorship as seasoned entrepreneurs. I also thank John MacArthur, Ian Charman, Jim Claunch, Allen Gilmer, Don James, Dr. Ira Kasper, Dr. John Lomonaco, Rick Marriner, Paul McIntyre, Peter Michaelson, David Reid, Gerbert Schoonman, Phillip Schotts, Darryl

Willis, Tim Wotton, and Osama Ziadeh. I also thank my executive coach, John Reed, and his wife, Perry Ann. I especially thank my former leader, Dave Redeker, who was the best male boss to work with and for—a leader who really understood the value of inclusion and gave me the opportunity of a lifetime to work with the BP executive team. I thank Micki Grimland for the countless hours on her couch having honest conversations that shaped me into a better wife, mother, and leader.

I thank my team. There have been many talented people involved in the launch and growth of Pink Petro. I am grateful to Mandy Asberry, Valeria Delgado, Jennifer Effendy, Tammy Feldman, Dan Friedman, Mary Johnson, Ruth Ann Johnson, Li Ha La, Josh Levs, Adrianna Lopez, Linda Lorelle, Traci Messina, Usha Menon, Elletra Parnell, Tricia Principe, Marianne Robak, Molly Reems, Hughie Rolle, Stacey Sanchez, Eric Shapiro, Dan Sills, Jen Simpson, Sharon Staffel, Cathy Steffek, and Elaine Wyrick. I thank each of them for their contributions through some of the toughest times we faced as a growing startup.

I thank the believers. I thank Halliburton and Shell for making the initial investment into Pink Petro, and I thank countless clients, colleagues, and supporters for believing in me and helping me shape my vision and sharpen my execution, especially Angela Knight, Ana Kopf, Jody Markopoulos, Jenny McCauley, Deborah Stavis, Debra Stewart, Christina

Sistrunk, and Geeta Thakorlal. I also thank Hether Benjamin-Brown, Meghan Nutting, and Marilee Norred for seeing my vision beyond Pink Petro. I also want to thank a mentor, Kathleen Eisbrenner, former Chairman, CEO, and Founder of NextDecade LNG, who passed away suddenly in 2019. I also want to thank another mentor, Doug Cain, former President of Lake Trucklines, who passed away from cancer in 2017 and was Pink Petro's first male member.

I thank my posse of purpose. To blaze a path, you need a village. That village is full of role models and people who care about driving the future for women (and) energy. I thank Yassmin Abdel-Magied, Reem Abdullah Al-Ghanim, Enass Abo-Hamed, Amanda Accardo, Tajuana Antwine, Amanda Barlow, Terri Bannister, Courtney Battle, Kari Blythe, Nicole Braley, Brandy Brazell Obvintseva, Laura Buss Sayavedra, Cheryl Chartier, Melissa Challenor-Bevis, Vicki Codd, Denise Cox, Stephanie Cox, Amanda Dasch, Pam Darwin, Sarah Derdowski, Alma Del Toro, Johana Dunlop, Shanta Eaden, Robin Eastman, Kathy Eberwein, Joan Eischen, Jamie Elrod, Samira Farid, LaDonna Finnels-Neals, Kera Gautreau, Heather Gillbanks, Paula Glover, Shara Hammond, Michelle Haradence, Arquella Hargrove, Jen Hartsock, Rita Hausken, Sonia Hernandez-Cordon, Jen Hohman, Hillary Holmes, Bonnie Houston, Jennifer Joffe, Janeen Judah, Jeanne Johnns, Deanna Jones, Tracy

Josefsky, Kim Jordan, Tracey Kearny, Eddie Kelleher, Susi Knight, Brandy Khoury, Kelly Lawrence, Angela Long, Susan Mann, Evelyn MacLean Quick, Regina Mayor, Julie Mclaughlin, Massiel Melo, Brianne Metzger-Doran, Rohby Mitchell, Lori Morales, Valentini Pappa, Tina Peters, Ali Piper, Anthea Pitt, Rebecca Ponton, Marti Powers, Ana Prata Fonseca Nordang, Judit Prieto, Nancy Prince, Leigh-Ann Russell, Jennifer Scotten, Maggie Seeliger, April Sharr, Jillian Sherburne, Kate Sherwood, Pranika Uppal Sinha, Sarah Smith, Missy Sowell, Erika Tolar, Kristen Underwood, Paula Waggoner, Souzi Weiland, Dana Wells, Oonagh Werngren, Stacey Weltmer, Kristy Whitaker, Kimberly Wilson, Lucie Wuescher, and Alyssa Volk. I also thank Shantera Chatman, Denise Hamilton, Khaliah Guillory, and Sara Selber Speer for opening my mind to new experiences. And to the countless organizations and networks that are shaping the energy workforce of the future, I thank especially the Shell Women's Network (WAVE), Women of Equinor, Halliburton's WISE, Baker Hughes, Enbridge, Colonial Pipeline, Aera Energy, Women of Oxy, ConocoPhillips, Chevron, Weatherford, Cheniere Energy WILS, Marathon Oil, the Women of Worley, American Association of Blacks in Energy (AABE), American Association of Petroleum Geologists (AAPG) American Energy Society (AES), American Gas Association (AGA), American Petroleum Institute

(API), American Wind Association (AWA), American Women Geoscientists (AWG), Clean Energy Education & Empowerment Initiative (C3E), Combined Arms, Consumer Energy Alliance (CEA), Lean In Energy, The International Energy Agency (IEA), The Oil and Gas Admins International (OGA), Pride Energy UK, Powerful Women UK, Society of Petroleum Engineers, (SPE), United States Department of Energy (DOE), United States Energy Association (USEA), Women of Renewable Industries and Sustainable Energy (WRISE), and the World Economic Forum Global Shapers (WEF). And to all colleagues I worked with globally, my days at BP and Shell were formative in what led me to leap and go for something bigger.

When the rain and "flow" came, I had so many people who came to help. I thank Jennifer and Ryan Fitzjarrald, Marianne and Jason Robak, and Chris Pratt and Jennifer Schneider for giving us a place to stay. I thank Jaime Dourren and Steve Cooley, who helped my family and many others in our neighborhood boat to our homes during the storm. After fourteen days of sitting water, I thank the gut team of my father, Lance, Matt, and Andrea Reynolds, Chris Pratt and Jennifer Schneider, Meaghan and JP Yorro, the Mormon Church helpers, and Cathy Steffek, who watched for looters. I also thank my sister Aimee and my brother-in-law Brian Michael, and my sister and brother-in-law Karen and Frank Skowronski, for taking care of Ally and Maddie. I also thank the many people who sent gift cards, supplies, meals, texts, cards, and love. To my Lean In community and so many others—friends and strangers—and their generous support to help us rebuild our home, I will be forever grateful. I thank our builder, Kim Huston, who stepped us through the process of rebuilding, and I thank the entire West Houston memorial community for their love and support, especially Cara Adams, Holly Hitchen, Sara Lou, Jennifer McKnight, Maria Sotolongo, Shannon Robinson, and the Hurricane Moms Memorial Facebook group. And of course, I thank the man whose name I will never know, who rescued my daughter and me from rising waters in our neighborhood when it was clear we had to leave. I will never forget his act of kindness and the other thankless acts from unknown Harvey heroes across the world.

I thank my book team. Big thanks to Rhoda and Eric Shapiro; Dara Beevas, my publisher; Alyssa Bluhm, my editor; and the team at Wise Ink Creative Publishing. I thank all who are in the book, read it, gave feedback, and share it.

I also want to thank some of the biggest thinkers, risk-takers, and leaders, whose actions validated or shaped and inspired me in some way. Thanks to Notorious Ruth Bader Ginsberg, Gloria Feldt, Annise Parker, Adam Grant, Seth Godin, Lord John Browne, Vicki Hollub, Lynn Elsenhans, Susan Kucera, and Jeff Bridges.

I offer so much gratitude to Sheryl Sandberg, who started the fire in my belly to "lean in" and was there in my darkest moments, reminding me why I needed to keep going. I thank Sheryl's right hand, Rachel Thomas, the Lean In Foundation team she leads, and the entire Lean In community, who remind me of why I get up every day: to do what makes me most afraid and change the world. Big thanks to Raena Sadler, Emma Roberts, Amanda Guzman, and the circles team. I especially want to acknowledge regional leaders and founders, Nur Afifah Mohamaddiah, Julene Allen, Ruchi Angrish, Linda Brandt, Erika Cashin, Judaline Cassidy, Elisa Charters, Anna Dapelo-Garcia, Tara Dawood, Mary Dove, Insaff Elh, Susan Freeman, Preethi Guruswamy, Hannah Kay Herdlinger, Debo Harris, Angelis Iglesias, Rashmeet Kaur, Sanya Khurana, Melody Mitchell, Payel Mitra, Nuala Murphy, Brittany Paxton, Maybelyn Plecic, Corine Sandifer, Ruchi Sharma, Erica Smith, Rain Stawar, Alisha Tillman, Eva Tucker, Rena Suzuki Wagner, and Sarah Willey.

I acknowledge you, the readers. The late Steve Jobs, CEO and Chairman of Apple, once said he wanted to make a dent in the universe and celebrated the "crazy ones." I acknowledge all whose voices and ideas have dented the universe and to those who read these pages with a fire in their belly to make change happen. Go and grow. The world needs you.

BOOK KATIE

Katie speaks on a number of topics including social learning and technology, cultural change, fearless leadership, and the gender and skills gap in energy. She's worked with corporations, associations, and teams across the world to put together purposeful in-person and virtual events, workshops, and learning. Katie's style is contagious, funny, and allows for meaningful multicultural, generational, and gender inclusive learning.

Katie speaks for a fee. You may book her at www.katiemehnert.com or call the office at +1 281-741- 5482 (Central Time Zone).

Previous engagements include Phillips 66, Shell, General Electric, Marathon Petroleum, Halliburton, Baker Hughes, United States White House on STEM, Panola College, UC Denver, Rice University, C-Suite Network, the Diversity Summit, Gastech, the Offshore Technology Conference, and the International Petroleum Technology Conference.

"By far the best keynote I've heard in a while!"

"Katie Mehnert is nothing less than ten breaths of fresh air: frank, fast-thinking, fun, fantastic. Her pointed pen and engaging ways leak a flair for life and work that is her very signature. She leaves an imprint. Correction: footprint."

"Katie Mehnert's authenticity makes for an amazing presentation. You won't be disappointed."

"As a true leader, Katie's power comes from her ability to influence people and earn their respect."